M000202842

TOKLAT

The Story of an Alaskan Grizzly Bear

TOKLAT

The Story of an
Alaskan Grizzly Bear

by

ELMA and **ALFRED MILOTTE**

illustrated by **Laura Dassow**

Alaska Northwest Books™
Anchorage • Bothell

Copyright ©1987 by Elma Milotte.
All rights reserved. No part of this book may be reproduced or transmitted in
any form or by any means, electronic or mechanical, including photocopying,
recording or by any information storage and retrieval system, without written
permission of GTE Discovery Publications, Inc.

Second Printing 1989

Library of Congress Cataloging-in-Publication Data

Milotte, Alfred, 1904-
    Toklat: the story of an Alaskan grizzly bear

    Authors' names in reverse order in earlier edition.
    Originally published: The story of an Alaskan grizzly bear.
New York: Knopf, 1969. With new ill.
    Summary: Describes a year in the life of a grizzly bear and her three cubs
in Denali National Park and Preserve and the plant life and other animal
species of the biotic community.
    1. Grizzly bear—Alaska—Denali National Park and Preserve. 2.
Mammals—Alaska—Denali National Park and Preserve. 3. Denali National
Park and Preserve (Alaska) [1. Grizzly bear. 2. Bears. 3. Zoology—Alaska]

I. Milotte, Elma. II. Dassow, Laura, ill. III. Title.
QL737.C27M55 1987   599.74′446   87-26910
ISBN 0-88204-325-7

Cover design by Shawn Lewis

Alaska Northwest Books™
A division of GTE Discovery Publications, Inc.
22026 20th Avenue S.E.
Bothell, Washington 98021

Printed in U.S.A.

To the late
Dr. Adolph Murie
who shared his
knowledge of the
wilderness as we
walked together
over the foothills
of Mount McKinley
and the tundra of the
Toklat River Valley

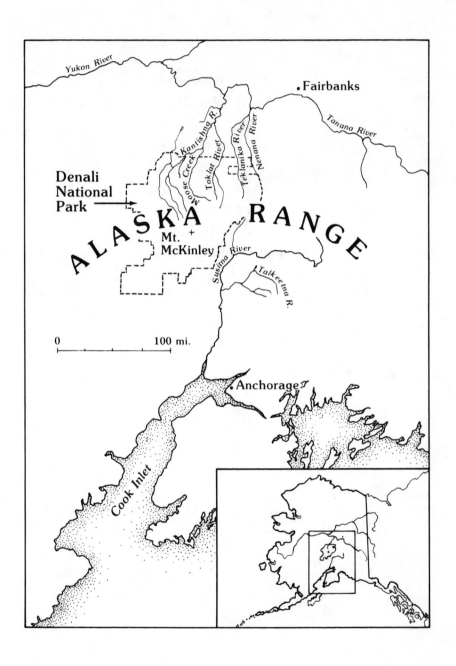

Yukon River

•Fairbanks

Tanana River

Kantishna R.

Moose Creek

Toklat River

Teklanika River

Nenana River

Denali
National
Park →

ALASKA RANGE

+ Mt.
McKinley

Susitna River

Talkeetna R.

0   100 mi.

•Anchorage

Cook Inlet

Contents

A green glow lights the evening sky. It is forty degrees below zero, and hidden in a den under the snow a mother grizzly sleeps through the winter with her young cubs. In another den, an ancient male grizzly lies frozen to death. He had not been able to catch enough food to keep him alive through the winter's semihibernation.

Much more than just a portrait of the life of an Alaskan grizzly, this book shows how each season brings different living patterns to the animals of the subarctic taiga — how caribou, beavers, wolves, mountain sheep, squirrels, mice, fish and birds maintain a fascinating ecological balance of a land of beautiful and terrifying contrasts.

Spring

The early spring morning was blustery. Choppy waters on the Gulf of Alaska tossed curls of spray onto the rocky shore. Here, on the tip of the Kenai Peninsula, a flock of twenty short-billed gulls rose, one by one, from the water. Following the western shore of Cook Inlet, they flew north on their annual migration to their breeding grounds at the foot of Mount McKinley two hundred and fifty miles away.

Leaving the broad salt-water bay behind them, they worked their leisured way up the Susitna River. Below them the spring sun had melted large, irregular patches on the snow-covered ground.

Guided by the peak of Mount McKinley, the tallest mountain in North America, the birds approached the Alaska Range. They crossed the glacial moraines, where gigantic snowfields and huge glaciers crept into the valleys and sent their melting waters into the streams and rivers.

For the gulls, the gravel bars of one of these rivers, the Toklat, were the end of their northward migration. Here in a subarctic environment, two hundred and fifty miles south of the Arctic Circle, they would make their nests and raise their chicks.

The headwaters of the Toklat River are not a sanctuary for the gulls alone. Wolf, caribou, ground squirrels, sheep, fox, and porcupine inhabit the alpine tundra, the forests, and the barren hills that surround the valley. Here, too, is the range of the Toklat grizzly bear.

In a den above the Toklat Valley, a grizzly bear and her three tiny cubs were about to finish their long winter sleep. Under a foot of snow, the entrance to the bears' den was hardly discernible and gave no clue to the pile of animals sleeping inside.

The mother grizzly, Toklat, had mated the previous summer, and alone in her den in the middle of winter had borne her cubs. At birth they were all the same size — about a foot long — and weighed a pound and a half each. Their eyes were closed and their ears were unresponsive to sounds. Even the sense of smell, one of their most valuable assets, showed no sign of development.

At first they had lain furless, buried in their mother's thick coat, suckling her warm milk. Hours went by with only the slow, measured breathing to indicate life in the squirrel-sized cubs.

Even in her semihibernating state, the mother had duties. Like a cat with a litter of new kittens, Toklat attended her cubs. With her long tongue she stroked and cleaned them. This bath, at times, seemed only incidental to the caressing, rubbing motion. She encouraged her young to wake up and come to a meal. The mother grizzly lay on her side most of the time, allowing the babies to assume a position at her stomach. They had their choice of nipples — the two between her hind legs or the cluster of four on her chest.

In about two months, the cubs had grown active enough to move about in the den. When hungry, they emitted whines, and when nursing, they made contented gurgling sounds.

The male was the darkest of the three cubs, with fur the color of rich brown chocolate. The larger female was growing a delicately colored jacket of straw-tan. The smaller female had a coat the color of a faded buttercup.

Toklat had dug her den on a slope that rose gradually

for a short distance, then met the base of a steep, rocky outcropping that towered two thousand feet above the Toklat River. Halfway up the cliff another series of rocks formed a jagged barricade that terminated in a sharp outline against the sky.

Now, between two of these huge columns, the sun had melted the snow and a flock of Dall mountain sheep grazed on the newly exposed dried grass.

Hidden deep in the snow beside the den, a field mouse, searching for a new feeding area, was digging a long tunnel from his nest. It twisted around several large boulders, where it barely missed the entrance to the grizzlies' den, then turned up the slope. The mouse pawed rapidly, trampling the pieces of loose snow into the floor of the passageway. He worked for several minutes, then he found a patch of lichens and stopped to feed.

Suddenly a distant booming sound reached his ears. He tried to determine the source of the noise. It did not come from any direction — there was nothing to run from. The sound became all enclosing, and then the earth trembled! The little animal became confused. He turned to run back through the tunnel, then stopped and turned again.

At the first shake, a great rock toppled from the cliff above and landed near the bears' den with a thunderous crash. Snow spewed out and joined the boulder as it rolled and rushed down toward the river bar.

This nearby heavy sound startled the little field mouse. His whiskers stiffened and twitched. His ears followed the direction of the noise as the rock cascaded downward.

Some of the loose snow tumbled into the den entrance, almost closing the tiny air vent that the warmth of the grizzlies kept open. The violent movement of the earth, and the accompanying sound, disturbed the sleeping bears. The cubs cried softly and pressed closer to their mother.

The mouse listened for a number of seconds, then scurried back through his tunnel. The stiff hairs on his nose trailed backward along the snow walls, the shorter ones probing the darkness before him. These delicate feelers told him instantly of any obstruction in his blind scurryings.

His movements were rapid, frenzied, as he slid through the cold blue pipe. But he soon found his passageway blocked by a wall of hard-pressed snow. Attacking it near the bottom with his slender claws, he made very little progress. Turning to his left, he found a tiny patch of softer snow. It fell away easily and was quickly packed into the floor by his stamping feet. In seconds he felt the snow wall give way before him and his head entered the grizzly den. Small snow bits hung on the ends of his whiskers. A shaking twist of his body tossed them off. His bright black eyes explored the den's interior. There was no movement. The bear family was again sleeping soundly.

The mouse slipped from the comforting security of his tunnel and slid down the wall into the den. In the dim light, he could see the bulky bodies towering over him. Part of the floor was covered with dried grass and small limbs of willow bushes that the mother bear had carried into the den in the fall. Avoiding this area, he ran rapidly along the right wall, where Buttercup slept against her mother.

The mouse hurried around the pile of fur and tried to find a place to hide. The sole of the mother grizzly's rear paw towered before him. Stopping a moment, he sniffed its strange odor, then scurried to a depression in the floor that had a ceiling of fur.

The fur belonged to the chocolate-colored cub.

In the warm darkness the mouse felt secure for the first time since the rockslide had frightened him. His tiny sides vibrated with each quick, short breath. Minutes passed and the mouse's fear gradually subsided. With his front paws he stroked his nose, pushing his whiskers forward. Then he stopped and listened. He could hear the slow breathing of the bears and beyond that, the whisper of wind outside the den.

With calmness around him, he again faced his problem of the morning — food. His nose crinkled, seeking a familiar odor, but in the riot of grizzly smells he only grew more confused.

Suddenly the pile of fur descended, pinning him to the earth. The pressure forced the air out of him and he gave a shrill squeal.

At the strange sound, Chocolate opened his eyes. Under the weight of the cub's leg, the mouse squealed again. The cry was muffled by the fur and only the one bear heard it. Then Chocolate raised his paw to scratch his ear and the tiny rodent raced across the rough floor.

The cub was too young to be interested.

The mouse saw the vent hole at the entrance of the den and ran toward it. Without stopping, he squeezed through the circle of light and disappeared.

As the morning sun rose higher, its warmth reached the level of the den. It started a trickle of water creeping under the snowbank. Wandering around the dormant grass roots, it seeped through a crack in the rocky earth to the chamber where Toklat and her cubs were sleeping. It slowly formed a pear-shaped drop, then detached itself from the den ceiling and plunked onto the fur of one of the cubs. Another sphere formed and dropped. Then another and another! Soon a thin, glossy, stringlike stream of water landed on Buttercup. It sank slowly through her fur and the coolness annoyed her. She climbed to the shelter of her mother's front leg.

Another trickle formed on the ceiling — ran away from the first, then dropped onto the mound of fur. The first watercourse became a steady stream, penetrating through the fur onto the mother's warm hide. She turned to escape this nuisance but her movement only spread the irritating coldness.

The moisture on the ceiling found several new channels, and fluid rods of icy water soon prodded all the bears.

Toklat awoke and swung her head from side to side, wrinkling her nose and drawing in short, quick breaths. No odor of danger reached her half-numbed brain, but the vague scent of spring sent an awareness through her. Food demands stirred her more acutely than the incessant streams from above.

She yawned and flexed her front paws. Water dripped off her long yellowish hair and formed a small pool under Chocolate. He moved around his mother to a drier spot.

When the sun reached the den's air hole, a bright ray probed close to the bears. Toklat half rose, half crawled toward the beam, toppling the cubs from her side. She paused with her head in the small shaft of sunlight. The glare bothered her and she blinked her eyes. Poking her nose into the tiny vent, she sampled the clean odors of the morning.

Toklat needed no calendar to tell her that it was spring. Her sensitive nostrils gave her clues to the awakening world before her. She stepped forward and, with several strong swipes of her front paws, shoved the snow away from the exit. The icy pieces tumbled, turned, and slid down the steep slope. Some rolled like balls and packed more snow on their surfaces, gaining in size with each revolution.

Toklat crawled through the opening and paused for a moment, sniffing the morning air. Still only half awake, she slipped on the snow and joined the miniature avalanche sliding toward the valley. As a cub she had often enjoyed the snowslides, but she had not planned this ride! Attempting to stop her downward motion, she flattened her body and spread her front legs out far on each side. Her back feet, with their wide, flat soles, were of no help in slowing her descent. Halfway down the slide she stopped kicking and pawing, and coasted to the bottom, where she stopped half buried in the loose snow. Regaining her feet, she gave a big shrug, sending the snow flying from her fur.

Suddenly a compelling odor reached her. A faint stench of decaying flesh floated across the slope in the morning breeze, and Toklat pointed her nose in its direction. She confirmed its source and without hesitating, turned, dug her long claws into the snow, and galloped rapidly back up the hill. The long yellow-brown fur on her back rippled with each powerful leap. She passed the den entrance without stopping. She was on the unseen scent-trail of food.

On a high peak, a Dall sheep watched Toklat as she crossed a narrow snowdrift and lumbered onto a slope of crumbled rock. At the far side, Toklat hesitated and swung her head to pick up the scent. Walking rapidly back onto the snow, she left a deep pattern of footprints behind her.

As she drew close to the base of the cliff, her nostrils worked constantly. Near the rock wall a leg and black hoof stuck out of the snow. It was an old ram that had died of starvation and had been buried by the winter storms. Toklat pulled the partially thawed carcass out of the snow and began her meal.

A marmot, sitting on the edge of the rock slope, saw the grizzly bear and whistled a long, sharp call. Feeling secure on his high ledge, he spread himself flat on a rock to enjoy the warm sun.

This was the first meal Toklat had eaten for six months. Her stomach had shrunk during her long fast, so she merely nibbled on the thawing food. Several times she paused to taste the moist snow.

When Toklat finished eating, she tried to cover the carcass. Straddling the dead animal, she pulled and scraped snow and rocks backward, first with one paw, then with the other. With greater determination, she used her front feet in unison, throwing the wet rubble between her hind legs.

Turning back toward her den, she left behind her a large reddish-brown mud scar at the edge of the snowbank. The sun's warmth still carried a strong scent into the air.

As she moved away, a flock of long-tailed magpies soared overhead, then dropped heavily onto the littered snow patch. Toklat stopped and, looking back, watched them land.

Moments later a red fox, with his nose high and his bushy tail straight out behind him, appeared at the base of the cliff. Catching the scent of food, he climbed the white bank and loped toward the odor. The magpies rose as a unit, their voices scolding back at the fox.

The fox found the food pile but Toklat turned and charged toward him. The fox retreated down the bank.

Toklat returned to the entrance to the den. She sat upright with her back anchored in the snow, and scratched her belly

with her long, curved front claws. As she scraped, she turned her head from side to side and made a happy grunting sound.

Inside the den the cubs heard their mother and stirred restlessly. Chocolate was the first to respond. He crawled across the puddle on the floor, tottered unsteadily to the exit, and disappeared in the bright sun. The two other cubs followed him through the opening.

Toklat sat farther back on her haunches and dropped her head toward the cub as he stepped into the sunlight. He moved toward her, but his wobbly feet slipped away beneath him. He instinctively dropped onto his stomach and slid down the bank.

Straw-Tan repeated the performance and in a pile of cascading snow joined Chocolate.

Buttercup followed her brother and sister and slid down the slope with all four legs straight out from her sides. She added a spinning maneuver to the descent, plus the squalling cry of a small, frightened cub.

Toklat watched them as they rolled down the hill, then she stepped forward, spread her front legs flat against the snow, and skidded down the bank to join them.

The cubs had been born three months before, but today was their first day out of the den. This was the beginning of a long period of alertness for Toklat and rigorous discipline for the cubs.

Mother grizzly regained her feet and shook the crusted snow from her fur. As she turned away from the morning sun, the rays outlined her body. She carried her head low between her shoulders. Her massive, high forehead was topped by two half-rounded ears. Her slender muzzle looked almost doglike as it drooped below her small, bright eyes. The hair across the bridge of her nose was short and pale cream in color. A hump of long hair behind her head gave character to every movement. The hump flowed over her shoulders and down her tapered front legs to her feet. At the belly line, the leg fur blended from cream to dark brown. Her hindquarters were supported by thick, stubby legs on nearly black feet.

The cubs gathered around their mother and found security in her nearness. She led them to a small knoll that dropped abruptly onto the edge of the wide river bar.

Toklat walked a few paces in front of the cubs and then waited for them. Her progress was slow, for she allowed the cubs to rest often.

The cubs' front legs bowed out sharply from their bodies and their toes turned slightly inward. Their hind legs were unruly. Each step was an awkward, uncertain movement, throwing the rears of their bodies from side to side as they floundered after Toklat.

The winding Toklat River had been hidden all winter under a rolling blanket of snow. The sun had already melted the thinner drifts, exposing rough bare spots on the riverbed. The remaining drifts were neatly smoothed at their edges. Small snow crowns poised defiantly on some of the rocks. The spring floods would soon turn the river into a wide, rushing torrent, but today only a partly frozen watercourse meandered through it.

Beyond the riverbed the rolling foothills changed into the steep, jagged contours of the Alaska Range. Farther to the southwest, the top of Mount McKinley towered 20,320 feet into the sky.

A breeze ruffled the fur on Toklat's hump, and her nostrils wiggled up and down, back and forth. The wind carried many messages. She analyzed them carefully for the odor of another bear or the strange scent of man. Suddenly a signal of danger reached her. Pressing her front feet against the ground, she shoved her body vertically into the air. The cubs instinctively recognized her alertness. Chocolate whined a note of fear. At this sound, his mother reached down and, with a swing of her front foot, sent him sprawling into the snowbank.

The protection of the cubs was dependent upon their silent obedience. Loving care was not enough now that they were away from the security of their den. They would have to be taught the necessity of instantaneous response to their mother's commands and actions. As cubs they would require this stern discipline to prepare them for their future safety.

Toklat again rose high on her short back legs and looked into the wind. Her front legs were bent against her body with the feet hanging downward like slender fingers. She held her head erect, her nose pointing into the breeze.

A hundred yards upwind, another mother grizzly bear, with twin two-year-old cubs, was digging roots at the edge of a snow island. Her rust-colored coat contrasted sharply against the white snow. The mustard-colored cubs wrestled and splashed in a trickle of water that ran from under the snow. The twins were almost as tall as their mother.

Toklat turned away from the strangers and galloped across a patch of snow onto a gravel bar. The cubs followed. Her run was not one of panic. Toklat's only concern was to maintain her family life without the intrusion of strangers.

Again she stood on her hind legs, looking back over her shoulder. Satisfied that they were not being followed, she dropped to the ground. She, too, began a search for roots.

The short dash had ended in a clearing where the sun had started to thaw the ground. With her right front paw, Toklat tried to dislodge the roots of a small shrub. Her claws could only scratch the surface. The food she relished was still frozen solid.

As Toklat and her family worked their way slowly across

the river bar, a small flock of short-billed gulls rose before them. Stopping on a low island, she tried again to dig, but she succeeded only in tearing up a stubble of roots. She chomped hungrily on these and moved on.

The first stream they came to was small but flowed strongly. Before crossing, Toklat again stood erect on her hind legs and, turning her head, sampled the wind currents. There was no danger, so she dropped forward and waded into the stream.

The water swirled around her legs and the long hair of her stomach trailed on the surface. In the center she changed her pace and with three splashing bounds reached the shore. She looked back at her cubs and uttered a guttural "rummmmpf."

As if on command, the cubs timidly entered the stream and struggled to make a crossing. The water rose high onto their backs and they half swam, half jumped to the shore. Chocolate and Straw-Tan were first across. Buttercup, caught in a strong current, floundered a moment in an eddy, then grabbed a flat boulder and climbed ashore. The cubs took turns shaking the icy water from their bodies before they gathered at their mother's side.

At the last high water, a small pile of branches had collected about the base of a dwarf willow. Toklat slouched her hindquarters onto it and twisted back and forth. The pile of twigs and sharp sticks acted like a huge brush, scraping through her fur. As she rubbed, she rolled farther onto her back, until at last she lay with all four legs swaying rhythmically above her. Her thick waistline became a soft hinge holding her body together. She lay there scratching for several minutes — head and nose extended to get every part of her back in contact with the comforting brush. Her loose, black-lipped mouth opened and closed in time with her twisting.

Buttercup and Straw-Tan flattened, spread-eagled, on the damp gravel bar and watched. Chocolate chased the end of a long branch which his mother's rolling was moving teasingly before him. Toklat, finished with her rubbing, turned and sat up on her haunches.

On a knoll above the river, a ground squirrel chirped. For a small animal he had a commanding voice. He had awakened from his winter sleep several days before and was resting in his tunnel entrance, soaking up the sun's warmth.

Seeing the grizzly family on the river bar below him, he ran forward several steps and rose onto his hind feet. Like the bear, he stood with his front legs tight against his body, his slender, long-toed feet hanging limply on his chest. His two back feet splayed out at a sharp angle from each other. He balanced with his tail curved onto the ground behind him. The fur on his underside was a brownish-gray. His back was darker, with long white guard hairs that grew in snowflakelike daubs. His head and shoulders were a yellow-brown. When he dropped back onto all four feet, his bearlike appearance ended.

For a moment, only the tip of his nose moved, then he drew his head down, hunched his shoulders, and sent out a warning signal. It was the sharp staccato note of immediate danger.

Almost before the sound had stopped, a second ground squirrel answered, then a third, and a fourth. The whole community was alert.

On a higher ridge, a marmot saw the grizzlies below, heard the squirrel's bark, and sent a whistle rolling across the valley.

Toklat ignored the rodents' calling and, followed by the cubs, continued her leisurely search for food.

The first rumble of an earthquake sounded far away, then it was everywhere, encompassing everything. The earth trembled. Toklat rose on her hind legs and, swaying unsteadily, drew in quick, hurried breaths, seeking the scent of danger.

Before her a sudden strong "whirrr" crackled out of the dry branches as a flock of white ptarmigan rose as a unit and circled away. Against the snowbank they were unseen, but as they rose into the blue sky, they fluttered like a handful of confetti swirling in the breeze.

The three cubs stopped and shrank back as if each had been struck an invisible blow at the same time. Chocolate stood erect, sideways to the sound, ready to run in either direction.

The sound of the tremor stopped as rapidly as it had started. Only the tops of the tallest spruce trees continued to sway. The quake had lasted fifteen seconds.

A red fox appeared on the far side of the thicket and trotted away. The quake had interrupted his stalk and spoiled his chance of getting a breakfast of birds.

Fifty feet in front of the bears, a flock of longspurs rose into the air, warbling. Their intricate song seemed to restore order to the tundra.

Toklat watched the birds and the fox for a moment, then, back on all fours, continued across the river bar. Before her the main channel swung in a large U, undercutting the bank and leaving a small, steep bluff. In unison, the bears stepped cautiously into the stream. As if on a signal they broke into a gallop, splashed through the icy water, and raced up the bank. It was a joyous motion and each tried to be first to the top.

Toklat sat and licked the sole of her hind foot. By fall, the pads would be thick and calloused, but today they were soft from months of disuse.

She rose and walked slowly through a tangle of dwarf birch, stopping occasionally to add the first new, swelling buds to her menu. She avoided a deep snowbank and entered the edge of a small stand of white spruce. The cubs tagged along single file, little Buttercup in the lead. She cried softly and the other two joined in the rough harmony. They had not nursed for two hours and now protested the long delay.

At a cluster of three spruce trees, Toklat stopped and sniffed at a scarred trunk. From it she drew the faint scent of another bear into her sensitive nose. The odor told her that it had been days since the stranger passed. She reared up on her hind legs and held the trunk for a moment with her right front leg. She nipped at the bark, then stretched both front legs as high as she could reach and sank her claws into the tree. She clawed twice and each stroke left deep, jagged gashes in the bark.

Satisfied with the long stretch, she turned and rubbed her shoulders against the trunk, moving only the upper part of her body. It was a rolling, back and forth movement, with her front legs waving before her in an awkward, balancing gesture. With her head far back, she rubbed the area between her ears. Next she dropped her front legs to her sides and bent her knees. Up and down she scratched her back against the tree. After scratching a few minutes, she sat back, making a soft sound in her throat. Her cubs crawled to her and suckled.

The red fox was still hungry. The earthquake had cheated him out of a ptarmigan breakfast, but he knew where there were other hunting areas.

He had not started to shed his winter coat. His thick red-tan fur concealed the movements of his hips and shoulders and contrasted sharply against the snow. His long legs were like dark shafts stuck into his body. His tail trailed straight out behind him.

Following down the stream until it narrowed, the fox was about to jump across when a movement in the water attracted his attention. A mouse, caught in the rising river, was trying to check his violent ride.

The fox watched, his pointed ears alert. The current carried the half-submerged mouse close to the shore. Fighting the force of the water, he was tossed against a slender root. Clinging to it for a moment, he pulled himself toward the bank.

The fox brought his feet close together and jumped. His first leap landed him midway across the stream. His second

leap landed him on the mouse. He reached into the water with his muzzle and brought up the dripping, half-drowned animal. Stepping out of the stream, he flipped the little creature into the air. He expected to catch it as it fell, but his wet feet slipped off the rocks. He lunged at the mouse but missed. The tiny rodent scampered under a cluster of thick roots to safety.

In the distance, a ground squirrel barked a warning. The fox crossed the snow and trotted leisurely but not without purpose. He ran a few steps, then stopped and listened. Cupping his ears forward, he could hear another mouse scurrying under the snow. The sound moved toward him and he followed its progress with a turn of his head. Again he silently positioned his feet and prepared to leap.

The mouse was about three feet in front of him when it

stopped. The fox cocked his head, waiting, checking his range, then he jumped. He made a high arc through the air and landed with all four feet on the snow over the mouse.

For several seconds neither hunter nor hunted moved. Then the mouse, pinioned under one of the fox's feet, tried to escape. The fox felt the movement and quickly plunged his sharp nose into the snow. Again he was unlucky! The mouse raced back into its nest under a heavy root.

Continuing his hunt for food, the fox entered a draw and walked carefully through the clumps of dwarf birch. This small, eroded valley separated the ground-squirrel area into two colonies. He turned right and stalked to the brow of the knoll, using the nearest cluster of birch for concealment.

Thirty feet before him three ground squirrels rested near their burrow entrances. The largest animal flicked his tail twice, then raced to his neighbor, who greeted him by sitting upright. The two animals boxed a moment, then the smaller

one tired and scurried into his tunnel. The third watched quietly.

The large squirrel dropped forward and bounded toward the brow of the hill, a route which would take him ten feet from the fox. The fox crouched, muscles tensed for the leap. Only the slight movement of his feet told of his intentions.

The squirrel rippled across the exposed grass. Stopping on all fours, he appraised the river bar. Tail high, he shouted a challenge into the air.

The fox sprang across the slope and cut off the squirrel's escape route. The squirrel dodged twice, but his tiny legs were no match for the fox. The contest was over in seconds. The fox, successful at last, trotted to his mate in the den, carrying the limp squirrel.

When the cubs finished nursing, Toklat rolled onto her feet and headed down the slope. The round-bellied cubs wobbled in a loose group behind her.

Chocolate, the most timid, stayed almost beneath his mother. Little Buttercup moved aside and with her mouth attacked a small branch which swayed from Toklat's passing. Straw-Tan followed meekly in her mother's broad footsteps.

Toklat led her cubs back and forth through the brush, smelling and poking at everything that might be food.

A mouse, in his nest under a clump of roots, heard the thumping approach of the bears. He stopped feeding on the grass bulb which he held in his paws, and listened. The thumping grew louder.

Toklat rolled a piece of sod toward herself, and the tiny world around the mouse collapsed in a squeezing clutch of darkness and earth. The bear's rough nose pried through the roots and gravel. Into her sensitive nostrils came the scent of the imprisoned rodent. She found it and with a lick of her tongue drew it into her mouth.

By midafternoon the grizzly bears had waded across

several streams to the opposite side of the valley. Toklat avoided the snowfields, preferring to walk over the freshly exposed tundra where deep caribou trails, edged with mounds of tough grass, were becoming visible as the snow melted.

In the west, a small caribou herd worked its way over the crest of a hill, feeding at each patch of lichens. This was the vanguard of the hordes of animals to follow.

Circling a deep snowbank, the caribou ran across the slope below the grizzlies. The herd moved as a unit, each animal trying not to be last in the group. Their actions seemed to synchronize as they slid haltingly down the bank, waded across the open water, and jogged onto the gravel bar. At times they quickened their pace, as if in a hurry to reach their trails on the hillside.

New antlers had started to appear on most of the bulls. Some had several inches of soft, black, velvety growth. Others had only the first stubby knobs indicating where long branches would soon develop. The cows carried their old antlers but would drop them after calving time.

One of the animals, an old male, lagged slightly behind the herd. At the stream crossings, he was the last to ford the water.

The herd entered a patch of willows and fed nervously. Some browsed on the thin branches while others pawed at the ground, loosening shafts of grasses and sedges for a sparse meal. Several fed on a bed of lichen and moss which peeked out from the edge of a snowbank.

The old male was the last to enter the feeding area. His head drooped and he coughed violently. A nostril fly had deposited its eggs in his nose and they had worked their way into his throat. As the larvae grew, they made feeding and breathing difficult. He coughed again to relieve the irritation, and made only a feeble attempt to eat.

The caribou herd left the patch of willows and trotted over a snowbank. The old male made no effort to follow.

Upriver from the caribou, a family of wolves rested outside the entrance to their underground home. The wolf parents had taken over the excavations made by foxes several years before. The foxes had dug a maze of dens and connected them with tunnels. The adult wolves had enlarged them for avenues of escape.

There were nine wolves in the pack. The black male and gray female had produced the litter of five pups, now yearlings, that played about the main entrance. An older female who had been born three years before, and a male who had been accepted by the group last fall, made up the rest of the pack.

The wolf family enjoyed the afternoon sun, which warmed the bare earth around their den. The black male lay flat on his side with both front and back legs crossed. The five pups, almost as large as their parents, lay on their stomachs facing one another and sparring roughly with their open mouths. A growling, rasping sound came from deep in their throats.

The mother wolf lay with her front legs before her, supporting her heavy head. Her sides had begun to bulge with a new litter that would be born in a month. Her mouth was open and her tongue pumped up and down in rhythm with her breathing. Her large gray ears, outlined with a fringe of short black hair, moved constantly. She relaxed them against her neck as a pup approached. He nuzzled his mother's black nose, then returned to the other pups. The mother dropped her head between her front legs and closed her eyes. The black skin line of her eyelids angled upward across her face.

For minutes she rested. Then a breeze carried the scent of caribou to her nostrils. She opened her eyes and, without

raising her head, checked the odors in the wind currents. In seconds the other adults picked up the same signal.

The scent was a prod to their actions. The black male rose quietly, stretched, then walked several steps down the slope to scan the river bar a hundred feet below. A quarter of a mile away, he saw the caribou herd cross the stream to feed in the willow thicket.

The gray mother made no attempt to move, but the other adults and the pups joined him. He acknowledged them with a quick dipping of his ears, then trotted through an opening in the brush and disappeared. The others followed, and on the riverbank they regrouped and loped toward the caribou.

They ran parallel to the waterway a short distance before attempting to cross. The male leader poised a moment at the water's edge, then leapt into the stream. He landed beyond midpoint and the force of the water carried him downstream. The crossing was never in doubt. He paddled strongly until his feet touched bottom, then with two bounds reached the top of the bank and shook himself.

The pack repeated the example set by the lead animal and reassembled on the bank. The eight wolves wagged their tails and nipped playfully at one another. Their greetings completed, the lead wolf ran toward the caribou. The wolves did not make a stealthy stalk, but depended upon their speed and strength to make the kill. The sick caribou, lagging behind the herd, was an easy victim.

They all fed silently for minutes, then the pups challenged one another for a choice morsel. Their yipping, throaty sound, rolling into the hills, alerted the rust-colored female bear and her twin cubs that Toklat had seen in the early morning. She knew the meaning of the wolf cry. Crossing the streams with a slow, rocking gait, she rolled her head from side to side, collecting the sounds and scents. The twin cubs galloped awkwardly behind her.

The big wolf was the first to see the grizzlies approaching and stood alert. One by one the rest of the pack saw the male's attentive pose and sprang to their feet to watch. Two pups stopped playing and faced in the direction of the intruders.

An eddying air current carried the meat odor to the grizzlies and they broke into a charge. Their loose, furry hides rippled across their shoulders with every bound.

The big black wolf made a quick spinning turn. Behind him, the younger animals began jumping stiff-legged about the partially eaten caribou.

The mother bear charged into the group and tried to strike the nearest wolf with her front paw.

She missed.

The wolves retreated and formed into a circle around the bears.

The mother grizzly sniffed the carcass and was about to take a bite when the black wolf attacked her flank. She turned and made a swipe with her front paw. Again she missed.

The female wolf approached from the rear and the grizzlies turned to meet her. For minutes, snorts, growls, and roars filled the air. Two of the yearling wolves were the first to withdraw. They moved away a few feet, then stopped to look back as they rested on their haunches. The black wolf soon lost interest in the game and ran into the brush.

A pup picked up a heavy piece of meat and tried to drag it away. The grizzly cubs made bluffing motions in his direction. The pup dropped the meat and ran after the disappearing pack.

The bears stayed at the carcass and fed for half an hour. When they finished, the mother dragged the remains to a nearby clearing and slowly clawed a rough pile of dirt, roots, and snow over them. This was no more than a token covering, for she left large portions of the kill still exposed.

The snow-covered top of Mount McKinley glowed a deep pink against the darkening sky. From his perch on a high cliff came the shrill cry of a golden eagle. At a distance another answered. They were watching the slopes below for food.

On the ground, a flock of ptarmigan scurried across the snow and vanished into a clump of willows.

Suddenly the male eagle dived toward the ground. He circled low for a moment, then with beating wings landed. Within seconds his mate joined him.

The eagles had sighted the caribou killed by the wolves and partially buried by the rust-colored grizzly bear. They sank their long talons into an exposed portion and with their heavy beaks tore out chunks of meat. They fed rapidly. When their meal was finished, the eagles hopped along the bank and became airborne. With slow, strong wingbeats, they soared in the air to their nest in the cliff above Toklat's abandoned den.

Toklat and the cubs did not see the drama played by the wolves and bear near the river. After climbing the hill they had wandered around a large snowbank and down a draw to a squirrel colony on the other side of the slope. Large areas of bare earth had been exposed by the spring sun and the ground squirrels were resting near their burrows. The first squirrel to see the bears barked a warning. A second animal answered and, as Toklat approached, dived into his den. Several long leaps brought the bear to the entrance to the squirrel's tunnel. She stopped, sniffed, then dug vigorously. Loosened rocks tumbled down the hill below her.

The squirrel heard the first digging sound and raced through an escape tunnel. The frightened animal quickly passed the side routes until at last the exit he sought

appeared before him as a spot of light. He stopped for a second with only his head sticking out of the tunnel. He saw the grizzly still working at the far entrance, but the bear's front quarters had disappeared in the hole she was digging. The squirrel jumped out of the exit and raced across the rocks to the burrow of another squirrel.

For a few minutes Toklat continued tossing pawsful of dirt and rocks out behind her, then, recognizing defeat, walked away. The spring day was almost over for the grizzly family. The cubs hung close to Toklat's side and poked expectantly against her stomach. She entered an open swale where clusters of willow and dwarf birch formed a soft barricade to her passage. She picked her way carefully through the brush, climbed over a snowdrift, and stopped under a group of spruce trees. An old tree, uprooted by the wind, leaned against its neighbor at a sharp angle, forming a natural shelter.

Sitting on her stubby tail, Toklat stretched her rear legs out before her. The cubs scrambled into her fur and each found a nipple and nursed.

In the tree above the grizzlies, an owl mother settled over her clutch of eggs to protect them from the chilling drafts which seeped through the nest's rough sides. She greeted the night with a gentle "Whoo — whoo." Another owl answered.

The sun had dropped below the horizon an hour ago and now the blue shadows of the Alaska tundra slowly melted together. The night sounds told Toklat of the increased activity of nocturnal prowlers. The she-wolf howled a long, mournful tone from her den on the knoll. Somewhere beyond, a pair of coyotes talked in high, shrill, happy tones.

The drip, drip, drip from under the snowbanks slowed, then stopped, leaving tiny ice fingers hanging from the underside of the arching drifts. In the freezing temperature, the night sounds seemed clearer and nearer. A slight breeze strummed its way through the slender spruce needles.

Toklat and her family snuggled together under the protective tree. The cubs, nestled in her fur, were only shadings of color marking their positions.

Summer

Three months had gone by since Toklat and her cubs had left the den. In their first weeks outside, the cubs had spent the dark nights in quiet restfulness at their mother's side. But as the days passed, the hours of sunlight grew longer, until now, in summer, there was no true darkness. In the evening the sun dipped toward the horizon, hid for several hours, then started to climb upward beginning another twenty hours of shining.

The sunrise was beautiful. Horizontal streaks of pink and golden-yellow fringed the bottom of every gray-purple cloud. The slopes of Mount McKinley picked up an edging of the same color. The cloud cover glowed overhead for minutes, then blended brightly into the crisp Alaska morning scene.

When Toklat left the den in the spring, her appetite had been dulled by the long semihibernation. Today her hunger was a constant thing and she searched continually for new food sources.

Here in the high tundra country spring comes late, but the long hours of daylight were speeding the growth of the vegetation. The sun had thawed the crust of earth above the permanently frozen subsoil and flowers were blooming everywhere. The first evidences of fruit were beginning to appear on the blueberry and buffaloberry bushes. The wild-pea vine and saxifrage plants were easily pulled from the ground, and roots, stalks and leaves were food for Toklat. Her staple diet, however, was the thick clumps of long grass that rippled in the summer breeze.

Headed in a northeasterly direction, the grizzly family followed the grass-lined edges of several small lakes and skirted the indistinct outline of a beaver pond. After a week of travel, they left behind them the streams which drain into the east fork of the Toklat River, and crossed over the lower slopes of Sable Mountain. Before them was the broad drainage area of the Teklanika River.

They succeeded in fording several of the smaller streams, but at the main channel the high water made a crossing impossible. Turning upstream, Toklat led the cubs through the bramble of willow, dwarf birch and blueberries. Her course was now back toward Mount McKinley and her familiar range at the head of the Toklat Valley.

This had been a leisurely trip and they had touched part of the outer perimeter of their hundred-square-mile range.

Every day the warming sun and rain encouraged grasses and shrubs to display their new growth. In early July, Toklat and her cubs were back in their favorite area — the Toklat River basin.

Its appearance had completely changed. The steep slopes were now covered with evergreen dryas, the oak-shaped leaves forming a green carpet. Patches of gaily colored flowers were beginning to appear, scattered over the landscape in yellows, pinks, purples and blues. The blooms displayed shadings of individual colors, or combinations of hues at their tips or at their bases. The blossoms of some plants gave no clues to the bright berries that would follow. There were tall, short, oval, and starlike flowers, some bold and daring, shouting their beauty. Others, tiny and delicate, showed their loveliness only to the nudging of an inquisitive breeze.

Toklat led her cubs onto a grassy flat to graze. She turned her head slightly sideways, tore a clump of tall grass from the ground, and chewed the long blades into her mouth.

The asterlike fleabane, with its lavender flowers, grew under her feet. Above her, along a caribou trail, masses of tall blue-purple lupine towered over the grass. Near the edge of a small lake, the dwarf matted growth of the lowbush cranberries displayed their clusters of pink blossoms.

Toklat grazed slowly down to the lake. The shoreline and shallow water were fringed with a blanket of white cotton-grass. The roots grew in thick clusters and each stalk carried a single downy head. The two-foot-tall plants almost hid the cubs as they trampled them underfoot in their dash to the water.

At the sound of the cubs' playful splashing, an Arctic tern rose from her nest on the far shore and circled above the bears. Suddenly she halted her forward flight and, with a rapid fluttering of her wings, hung over the cubs, watching and scolding.

Chocolate and Buttercup stood on their hind legs facing each other and boxed. Buttercup soon lost her balance and toppled backward, the water closing over her. She splashed back onto her feet and joined Chocolate in a race to their mother.

Toklat and Straw-Tan grazed into the cottongrass, then both animals sat upright in the shallow water.

In the air above them, several other birds soon joined the lone tern. They soared, dived, and scolded the bears below them. These Arctic terns had arrived a month before, completing a twenty-two-thousand-mile annual migration to the Antarctic and back. Called the "greatest sun worshippers," they experience more hours of daylight than any other creature.

One by one the birds glided back to the hummocks of withered grass at the shore and resumed their nesting. One of the terns settled forward onto her breast and, kicking backward, soon formed a small depression beneath her. In

several minutes her nest was finished. Around her, other terns rested quietly. Under one bird a pair of mottled olive-green eggs was about to hatch. In another nest, two downy chicks peeked out from their mother's pearly gray feathers.

The adult terns wore black caps on their heads. Starting at the nostrils, the black feathers dipped under the eyes and ended on the backs of the necks. As they sat on their nests, their long wing tips were crossed gracefully over their tails.

At the water's edge, a dozen birds stood facing into the breeze that rippled across the lake. Tiny wavelets splashed against their short legs, but the terns remained as motionless as white wooden decoys.

In the air over the middle of the pond, a male bird dipped and soared, then hovered over a small fish in the water below. For seconds he hung suspended, then dived, tipping the surface with his red bill. Kicking the water, he came up with a tiny flopping fish. Returning to the shore, he landed and walked to his nest. With wings extended he offered the morsel to his mate.

Mother Toklat galloped into the lake. The three cubs splashed along beside her for a short distance, but as the water deepened, they turned and followed the shoreline toward the hummocks where the Arctic terns were nesting.

On the opposite side of the lake, a cow moose alertly watched the noisy bears. Standing beside her were twin calves. One of the calves awkwardly folded his front legs and dropped to the ground to rest. Confident of his mother's protection, he lay quietly on a carpet of ground dogwood spotted with greenish-white flowers.

As the bears came closer, the moose moved several steps forward, instinctively placing herself between her calves and the danger. She held her bulbous nose high and ears forward to record the bears' progress. She stood almost motionless. Only her ears continued to turn and listen in

all directions. Suddenly her head swung to her right — her ears cupped to strengthen a new sound.

A hundred yards upwind, a huge grizzly bear limped out of the willows and stood at the edge of a clearing. The scent of the bear carried across the water to Toklat. For a brief moment she rose out of the lake and stood on her hind legs. With a muted "whoof" she dropped down and galloped through the terns' nesting ground. The birds directly before her flew away with frightened calls.

The three wet cubs trailed close behind Toklat. In Chocolate's footprints a mixture of cracked olive-green shell and egg yolk seeped into the trampled grass.

Behind them, across the lake, the stranger with an off-white coat limped slowly onto the flower-covered flat. It was Kluane, a very old grizzly bear who was migrating into the area from the south. The reason for his journey had occurred three days before, on the bank of the Chulitna River. The melting glaciers of Mount McKinley and the Alaska Range drain southward to the Chulitna River. Its waters join those of the Skwentna, Yentna, Kahiltna and many others, to form the Susitna, which empties into Cook Inlet.

On the skyline above the Chulitna River, the shadows on Mount McKinley's white slopes had blended together into a towering monochrome of gray-blue.

In the river, two grizzly bears stood belly deep in the shallow edge of a pool. In the water flowing past them, a series of sharp, pointed waves moved across the surface. They were created by the dorsal fins of king salmon working their way toward their spawning grounds. These latecomers, stragglers from the large schools which preceded them earlier in the summer, continued to struggle upstream. Seen through the translucent water, the fishs' bright-red sides were a muted pink.

One of the bears lunged into the deeper water and disap-

peared. Seconds later his head bobbed to the surface holding a fish securely in his mouth. The salmon did not move. The bear's powerful jaws had crushed its back.

He carried the salmon to a flat rock. Holding it with a front paw, he ripped long fillets off the side and ate them with a chomping motion of his lower jaw.

The second grizzly found a fish in the shallow pool and with a quick thrust of his head, picked it out of the water. He started toward the bank with his catch, when a flurry of frightened salmon disturbed him. He dropped the fish from his mouth and charged after the school. He missed all of them. Stepping onto a rock, he sat down in the slow current.

Upstream, a crashing in the brush alerted the two bears. They turned their heads and watched a third grizzly walk slowly out of the shadows.

It was Kluane, the large male with the thick, heavy head and coat of off-white fur. He was making a low, groaning sound because every movement of his mouth was painful. Years before, a bullet had fractured his jaw and he still carried it in his skull.

He stepped forward into a pool full of salmon and waited. The fish moved away at the touch of his legs but soon reassembled beneath him. They swayed their tails back and forth in a lazy, rhythmical movement. A big salmon, twice as large as the rest, worked its way up a riffle and into the bear's shadow.

Kluane opened his mouth and lunged at the fish. The bear's dripping head came up holding the seventy-pound salmon. The slippery fish twisted rapidly up and down, tossing a spiral of water into the air, its red sides flashing in the evening sun. The salmon's strong snapping movements were soon successful and, still flopping, it dropped into the water and raced away. The old grizzly made no attempt to pursue it.

Within seconds other fish assembled in the pool. Kluane repeated the plunge and came up holding a smaller salmon by the tail. Only the fish's head and body could move and it flopped slowly back and forth with a jerky, hesitant movement. The undulations were not rapid, but with every twist it worked farther out of Kluane's dull teeth.

The bear felt the fish slipping and raised his front paw to his mouth in an attempt to hold it. He was too late! The salmon dropped into the water. He took several leaps toward the escaping fish and with a front foot pinned it to the bottom. Slithering out of Kluane's grasp, the salmon splashed into the main channel of the river.

Kluane opened his black lips and huffed twice. Behind his lips was the reason for his unsuccessful fishing. A jagged row of yellow-black stubs lined his jaws. These were the last remnants of his once sharp, strong teeth.

The sun had dropped behind Mount McKinley and the somber blue hues of twilight deepened.

Kluane waded to the bank and followed a well-worn trail upriver. He turned onto a gravel bar covered with a thin sheen of water, each step shattering the stream's luster. His reflection in the water crinkled and swirled in a constantly changing pattern. Delicately carved designs of yellows and purples, with an infinite variety of shapes, floated before him on the restless stream.

Suddenly Kluane caught the dreaded scent of man. He stood high on his hind legs and pointed his black nose into the eddying wind currents. His nostrils worked up and down.

As he waited uncertainly in the water, a bullet entered his shoulder with a soft "PUFFFFFT" — it passed through and ricocheted into the scrub with a diminishing whine.

Kluane felt the bullet with more fear than discomfort, but in a split second the sound of the rifle snap reached him. This he remembered well! He swung around and in terror raced wildly away, and as he ran a second shot whined over his head — "PRRRREEEEEE."

The fleeing grizzly galloped along the swampy bear trails, crossed several streams, and plunged through a thicket of willows and small birch trees. He ran in panic for several miles. When the fear subsided, Kluane resumed his normal slow walk with only the pain in his shoulder to prod him onward.

He waded up a creek lined on both sides with devil's club. The plant's slender, angular shafts rose five feet above the bear, and were covered with long, sharp spines. Each plant had huge, two-foot-wide leaves along the trunk and a cluster at the top. Kluane crashed into the thorny barricade, heedless of the plant's stinging probes piercing the soles of his feet and his tender nose.

For two days Kluane climbed, and on the morning of the third day he reached the top of the divide separating the southward-flowing waters of the Susitna River from those of the Toklat River. This was his first trip over the summit of the Alaska Range and he would never again return to the Susitna.

Kluane had no way of knowing that he was entering the huge wildlife sanctuary which surrounds Mount McKinley, and that here he would be protected from hunters.

As he started down the slope his injured shoulder was forced to carry more of his weight. His limp became more pronounced.

With each step he crushed the carpet of Arctic poppies whose clear yellow heads balanced daintily on slender stems.

A flock of wheatears skittered and bounced into the air before him, their white rump feathers flashing with every move.

Stopping to rest, the bear sampled a clump of yellow cinquefoil blossoms.

At the foot of the slope, Kluane approached a small lake. A breeze picked up his odor and carried it across the water. On the shore, a hundred yards away, a mother moose reacted immediately. Her nostrils expanded and contracted. Seconds later the breeze shifted and the scent reached Toklat and her cubs. With several bounding leaps, the bears raced out of the water and onto the matted grass of the tundra. The Arctic terns rose into the air, scolding loudly.

The adventures of the morning had been exhausting, so Toklat found a grassy depression near the base of Sable Mountain to rest. Their bed area quickly became a mass of trampled grass and its sweet smell seemed to act as a drug to the tired bears.

Toklat was constantly disturbed by the ever-present odors and scents carried past her nostrils by the vagrant breezes. The cubs had not yet learned the need for alertness and slept contentedly near her.

Chocolate was the first to stir. He rolled onto his back and scratched his stomach with his front paw, then awkwardly with his back foot. Jumping to his feet, he made three leaps toward his dozing mother and landed on her neck.

Toklat enjoyed the cub's antics and leaned her head toward him with a rubbing movement. Chocolate responded and attacked his mother's ear with his mouth. The scuffling sounds awoke Buttercup and Straw-Tan and they both joined in the uncommon game with their mother.

Buttercup clawed her way up and over Toklat's back and landed in a rolling heap on the far side. Righting herself, she leaped back and buried her mouth in the long fur of Toklat's hump. It was a roughhouse game and the cubs played it with complete abandon.

Toklat curled onto her back and with a gentle swipe sent Straw-Tan tumbling from her side. Toklat's display of playfulness was so rare that the cubs acted as if they had found a new friend.

Chocolate and Buttercup jumped onto their hind legs, met head on, and boxed. Toklat rolled back onto her stomach, pinning a squalling Straw-Tan beneath her. Chocolate stopped boxing and Buttercup teetered toward her mother's head, her front legs flailing. Toklat, with a touch of her big paw, held the cub to the ground where she wiggled helplessly.

The game lasted only minutes and it was Toklat who canceled the fun. She rose to a sitting position and huffed a command. The cubs knew its meaning. Their mother's unusual relaxation had ended.

Toklat climbed to the top of a knoll. To her right she saw a herd of Dall sheep coming toward her. There were twenty sheep in the flock and they were crossing the valley toward the high cliffs of Sable Mountain. Most of the sheep were ewes followed by young lambs. They walked over the tundra single file and dropped down onto the rocky riverbed. Every move betrayed the animals' inner anxiety. One of the lambs jumped stiff-legged into the air and ran a short distance from his mother, turned, and raced back to her side. Here in the open flat their only protection was their alertness.

A yearling ram raced to the head of the column, saw Toklat, and stopped.

Toklat and the cubs walked into a small depression and were temporarily hidden from the sheep's vision.

The ram stepped forward and stamped a front foot. He was annoyed! As long as the grizzlies could be seen he had watched them with fascination. But, when the bears suddenly disappeared, it was too much for his courage. By his stance, he sent a warning signal through the flock. All the animals stood alert and watched until the bear family reappeared. One by one the sheep turned and, circling, continued toward the mountain.

Now their manner of walking changed. Carefully they selected a place for each hoof. Their jerky steps looked awkward and uncertain.

The steep base of Sable Mountain was a hundred yards ahead of the sheep. When the lead ram reached the slope he broke into a gallop and raced up it. With green vegetation under their feet, all the animals gained new confidence and soon the entire flock was playing follow-the-leader to the mountain. With their heads pulled back high over their shoulders, the sheep looked like a line of soldiers running at attention.

A young lamb broke from the line and picked his own way

up the trail. A pair of lambs bounced close to their mother's sides like balloons towed on elastic strings. As they reached higher ground the climbing became more difficult, but none of the sheep hesitated at even the roughest parts of the trail. The lambs' vitality was endless. As the flock entered the sharp, tumbled rocks, the lambs leaped up them with ease.

Within minutes, the sheep assembled on the jagged outcropping and each animal found a favorite spot to rest.

Between the bare pinnacles of rocks, patches of evergreen dryas covered the ground. From their dense clusters of leaves, long, slender shafts supported yellow flowers which were almost closed. In some clumps, a few blossoms had changed into fluffy plumes.

The yearling ram, whose appearance was almost identical to the ewe's in body size and horn growth, walked away from the rocks and onto the nearby tilted pasture. The strong herding instinct of the animals drew the flock, one by one, after him into the grazing area.

One of the ewes did not join the flock. She worked her way carefully up through the rocks until she found a small, isolated depression. Scraping the stones backward by pawing the ground with one front foot and then the other, she made herself a bed. Circling once, she folded her front knees under her and sank onto the softened earth. An hour later her lamb was born.

Above the ewe, a flock of ten rams was resting near the base of a sharp outcropping. Living apart from the ewes, the rams would remain on the higher meadows and rocky ledges during the summer months. A twelve-year-old stood on a point of rock, watching every movement in the Toklat Valley below. His front feet were inches from the edge. Standing with his hind legs slanted back at a sharp angle, his head projected out over the cliff. The sentinel's profile against the sky outlined his sturdy horns, which curved up

51

and back from the top of his head, made a circle, and stopped in slender points ahead of his eyes. When he looked directly to his side, he had to peek over the upward arc of each horn. The great size of these horns marked him as the oldest in the flock. He would carry them for life and not shed his horns every year like the moose, deer, and caribou.

Behind the patriarch, a young ram rested. His horns made only a short half-moon arc, with the tips pointing downward.

In the west a mass of clouds crept toward the Alaska Range. As the storm advanced, the highest peaks and glaciers slowly lost their crisp white outlines and acquired the blue-gray color of the storm clouds. The far earth-shapes disappeared, and the world, for the sheep, shrank to a small, hazy area a few feet around them.

As the first drops of rain started to fall, the damp cloud blanket seemed to press the flock together. Their safety from predators depended upon their seeing them at a distance. With visibility reduced to a few feet, the sheep grew nervous and walked toward the rocky cliffs. Each animal relied on his neighbor to warn him of danger and, in their shrunken world of drifting rain clouds, they moved in a closely packed group. One by one the sheep were absorbed by the fog.

A driving rain dropped through the mist and filled every depression with water. There were few places for it to rest in pools, so it rushed impatiently toward the valley.

The mother ewe with her new lamb watched as the flock was enveloped in the clouds. Soon she was alone in the storm with her baby. Shaking the rain from her body, she drew her head back between her shoulders. Holding this posture of apprehension, she looked about her, then slowly lowered her head to nuzzle her lamb.

He was now two hours old — a wet white bundle resting in the mud beside her. His mother's prodding nose aroused

him and he struggled to get his tiny black hooves beneath him. On the third try he rose waveringly. She moved several steps away, enticing him to test his legs. He stood a moment, then took his first step. Both front legs collapsed and he dropped to the ground with a wet splash. Without resting, he regained his feet, wobbled up to his mother, and had his first meal. In minutes, both the ewe and her lamb were enclosed in the cold, gray fog cloud.

With the start of the rainstorm, Toklat had led her family into a heavy growth of spruce. The roots of one of the trees, growing over a rocky ledge, formed a small shelter. A mother porcupine waddled out of the opening and started eating the leaves and branches of the buffaloberry.

Chocolate saw the porcupine and ran toward it. As the cub approached, the spiny animal turned her back and erected her defense. The quills across her hips rose like a wave and pointed forward. Those on her shoulders pointed up and backward. Meeting in the middle of her back, they formed a sharp ridge of interlocking spines from side to side. She tucked her nose between her front legs and waited. With her bright, round eyes peeking over her feet, she watched the cub approach.

Chocolate stopped for a moment near the porcupine and sniffed. The scent was not new, but the animal's appearance perplexed him. He made a slow circle around her. The porcupine turned with him, always keeping her tail and back pointed at the bear. The cub had come upon this scent before and had no memory of unpleasantness. He had found it in willow clusters, drifting down from tree trunks, and along his mother's bear trails. But this time the scent was strong — and it moved!

Chocolate stepped timidly toward the arc of yellow-brown quills and hair, raising his front paw to feel them.

"Swish" — the porcupine's eight-inch-long tail slapped against the cub's paw, driving a dozen barbs into the tender pad and toes.

Chocolate squealed in terror.

Toklat heard the cub's cry of distress and rushed to his defense. Chocolate ran a short distance, but with each step the quills sank deeper into his foot. Sitting down, he tried to lick the spines from his paw with his rough tongue.

Toklat swung her head from side to side, seeking the cause of her cub's alarm. She picked up the porcupine's scent.

Still huddling against the ground, the porcupine peeked over her front legs as Toklat approached. The angry bear lowered her nose.

"Swish — swish!" The sharp-spined tail struck twice in rapid succession.

Toklat roared and recoiled from the stinging pain of several dozen quills stuck in her nose and lips. She swung her forefoot over her muzzle, trying to brush away the annoying objects. The gesture drove some of the barbs deeper and broke the shafts of others, leaving the points embedded in her flesh. Roaring and grunting, she walked into a patch of tall willow, still trying to wipe the quills from her face by swinging her head from side to side. She sat and scratched her face with her hind foot, but only broke more quill shafts. She rose and, with a rumbling call in her throat, ambled toward the river. Straw-Tan and Buttercup jolted along beside her. Chocolate sat licking his paw, but when the other cubs left he hobbled after them on three feet, his fourth paw barely touching the ground.

The storm droned on, the rain beating with a strumming sound on the grass, leaves, and animals.

The porcupine remained motionless for minutes after the bears left, then slowly lowered her long hair and quills and waded through the wet grass to her den. Before entering she raised her dark, blunt head and shook the water from her back, then waddled into the dark cavity under the roots.

In the back of the small den her baby was sleeping. Its back and tail were covered with black hair and its short quills were starting to harden in the air.

The storm lasted until early afternoon. When the sun broke through the clouds, it found the tundra and mountains bathed in a new sparkling freshness. The lupine was decorated with large and small spheres of water that stood up from the surface of the leaves like transparent glass balls. These jewellike drops reflected in their domed roofs a distorted replica of the entire sky.

The rain waters had quickly collected in the small streams and were tumbling toward the largest river.

In the grass along the banks, several short-billed gulls had built their cup-shaped nests. Some lined them with moss and several had stuck preening feathers around the rims. Others had chosen the higher gravel bars, where they built nests of dry rootlets and sticks amid small piles of driftwood.

Toklat and the cubs were taking a path that was bringing them very near the bank nests. Two of the birds sank low, hoping to avoid detection. With their white heads and pearly gray backs, they were still quite conspicuous.

A short distance upstream, a flock of four gulls flew low over the willow brush, seeking ptarmigan eggs. They cocked their heads from side to side as they peered intently into the shadows. Suddenly they saw the bears approaching their colony and returned to defend it.

Other gulls, sitting quietly on grassy hummocks hunting mice, rose into the air and flew directly at the bear family. They made intricate dives, turns and banks, and scolded the oncoming bears with loud mewing calls. The birds' daring displays were successful and the bears passed the nesting birds without seeing them.

Toklat and her family wandered over two small ridges near the edge of a muddy stream. She was tormented by the quills in her face. Several more shafts had broken off, leaving the barbed points still embedded. In the rough black skin of her nose, two long quills protruded, forming a slender white V which danced constantly before her eyes. She tried to scent a ground squirrel in its burrow, but with every probing movement of her nose the barbs were forced deeper. Walking to a patch of tall grass, she found that grazing was less painful to her nose.

Straw-Tan and Buttercup were not involved in Chocolate's and Toklat's discomfort and followed playfully near their mother.

After a half hour of grazing, Toklat rolled onto her back in a clump of grass and swung her body back and forth. The cubs moved expectantly closer, and when Toklat

stopped
her wild gyrations,
they climbed to her
side and nursed.
When the cubs finished feeding, Toklat led
them down to a small, rushing stream. Feeding
along its bank, Toklat gulped mouthfuls of horsetail
grass, one of her favorite foods.

The grizzlies followed the water's edge until they came
to a beaver dam. They made no attempt to climb the three-
foot-high wall but walked past its downstream face, splashed
through the water at the base of the spillway, and went up
a low bank.

A young male beaver entered the pond from the upper
stream and stood quietly on a pile of mud on the bank, where
he left his strong castoreum scent. He rose onto his hind
feet, using his broad, flat tail for balance. With his front feet
tucked under his chin, he put his head back and sniffed the
air about him. He was migrating through this strange beaver
territory, seeking a new home. He dropped forward and
waddled into the water.

A breeze rippled across the pond, carrying the beaver's
scent to Toklat. She saw the beaver's back as he glided
through the quiet pond, his webbed feet shoving him
through the water with slow, powerful strokes. Sculling his
black tail strongly to the side, the beaver swam to the shore.

He crawled slowly up the bank, left his scent again, and re-entered the water. By the time Toklat reached the end of the small lake, the strange beaver had visited the bank three times.

The pond beavers' lodge was ten feet from the shore. The pile of sticks and mud protruded three feet above the surface. Inside the stack of limbs and branches was a small, dry cavity, the animals' sleeping chamber. The rough stick floor was several inches above the pond water level, and cemented with dry mud. Discarded bark, wood chips, and large splinters formed a carpet. Near one wall a circular pool in the floor was kept clear of sticks. This was the hatch through which the beavers entered the outer pond.

Against the far wall, a pair of beavers slept with their tails beneath them. Creatures of regular daily routine, the house beavers would not ordinarily awaken until the sun was near

the horizon. The pungent odor of the young beaver floated across the water and a small wisp of it sank through the barred vent in the ceiling of the lodge. This caused the animals to stir. The male poked his nose between the lower logs in the vent. The scent was unmistakable — an unwelcome beaver had arrived.

Sliding into the water-filled hatch, he felt his way through the dark tunnel until he emerged into his bright green underwater world. Two trout swayed slowly near the exit, and above him a muskrat paddled across the pond's surface. He knew both fish and rodent and accepted their presence.

Swimming rapidly through familiar underwater channels, he neared the shore and cautiously rose to the surface with only the top half of his head showing.

He again picked up the scent and trailed it to the shore. With the closeness of the intruder his anger rose and, with no thought of caution, he hurried up the bank where the beaver had left his last scent. He sniffed, then standing in a praying posture, he scanned the pond and shore. On his right he saw the bears sauntering toward him, but he was not alarmed. He had seen bears before and his escape route was always near.

An arrow-shaped ripple cut through the water. This was the sign of the intruder he sought. He watched for a moment until the young beaver walked up the bank.

The lodge beaver dropped forward and slipped into the pool. Normally he moved with a quiet calmness, but now his actions betrayed his mood. With strong strokes he shoved himself through the water. His webbed feet expanded with each backward thrust — contracted with the reach forward. He raced after the newcomer, his nose forming the tip of an arrowhead of waves trailing backward on each side.

When his feet touched bottom, he splashed out of the water and charged up the bank toward the trespasser. The intruder turned, saw his attacker, and tried to escape past him. The pond beaver sank his teeth into the loose skin of the interloper's shoulder and was towed back down the bank. There they tumbled and twisted in the shallow water.

Fifty feet up the shoreline Toklat heard the conflict. Standing on her hind legs, she saw the turmoil ahead. She dropped to the ground and galloped toward the beavers just as they submerged into a deeper area. When she reached the beavers' battleground, only a widening band of ripples and a small patch of muddy water told where they were. She splashed into the pond.

Near the bank behind her, the three cubs came to a halt and watched the chase.

The water was halfway up Toklat's side and she tipped her head trying to peer below the water's crinkly surface.

The two beavers struggled on the bottom, the older, heavier animal clinging to the younger trespasser. Suddenly they rolled rapidly, sending a new cloud of silt billowing out around them. The bear's legs were only two feet away. The pond beaver flipped his tail and it rose upward. For a second it flashed before the bear, then sank again into the silt. Toklat saw the movement and it was enough! Raising both front feet out of the water, she pounced down, trying to pin the beaver to the bottom. The claw on her right foot came down on the tip of the pond beaver's tail and pierced his leathery skin. Surprised and alarmed at this sudden attack from another source, he opened his jaw and released the stranger. For a second the invader floated on his side, then, realizing he was free, kicked backward with both hind feet. This shoved him out of the silt cloud and into the clear water.

Toklat felt no movement underfoot, so when she saw the beaver escaping, she lunged at him — but missed. The lucky trespasser swam rapidly away and hid beneath the branches of a sunken tree.

The pond beaver, now released, paddled to the deeper water and quickly found an underwater avenue leading toward his lodge. He had taken no air since the start of the conflict and reluctantly he rose upward. Using his tail for balance, he stopped swimming and broke through the surface with just the tip of his nose above water. He took a deep breath. With his lungs refreshed, he allowed his body to float higher, exposing his eyes and ears. One kick of his hind foot sent him into a slow, revolving circle. He could see the cubs on the shore, and Toklat standing waist-deep in the water, seeking a new clue to the beaver's whereabouts.

For a moment curiosity held the beaver at the surface, then with a slight arch of his back he raised his tail into the air and brought it down flat on the water — "whack." This gesture of defiance was also an aid to his dive, for with this signal he disappeared.

Toklat waded in the direction of the splash. When she reached the area, she tried to see through the rippling water. The cubs followed a short distance behind and watched as Toklat climbed onto the beaver's lodge.

The beaver had entered the underwater tunnel and, using his front feet, pulled himself up into the dim chamber. He touched his mate's nose with his, then listened a moment for any sound of pursuit. It was not long in coming.

The quiet of the beavers' house was shattered as Toklat climbed up the pile of sticks, limbs and mud. The smaller twigs broke under the bear's great weight, while the larger sticks merely creaked and groaned.

On top of the lodge Toklat carefully worked her tender nose between the branches.

Both beavers heard the huffing and puffing two feet above them. They sat quietly, trusting in the security of their house. They had heard sniffing and scratching sounds on their roof before and it had always withstood the attack. They made no sound to reveal their location, but another clue betrayed them. Their warm bodies sent currents of scented air streaming up through the vent, and the bear's sensitive nose found them.

Toklat started digging, sending clumps of mud and branches flying into the pond behind her. The material on the tip of the lodge yielded easily but as she dug deeper, her progress slowed. She now encountered a layer of green willow, which had taken root in the damp walls. This formed a tough living barricade between the bear and the beavers. Her temper, already short from the annoyance of the quills in her nose, mounted at the stubborn resistance and she challenged the problem with a roar.

"Rooorr — huff — huff — huff!"

The sound shattered the beavers' courage. They slid forward into their water exit and disappeared into the under-water world their dam had created.

Toklat's powerful digging quickly broke through the last obstruction and she lowered her head into the beavers' living quarters. Nothing but the odor remained! Stepping carefully down from the loose rubble of the house, she waded back to her cubs who waited restlessly on the shore.

"Smack." The triumphant sound of a beaver's tail hitting the water raced across the pond. "Smack." A second beaver answered from somewhere in the water grasses.

It was two hours before midnight and the sun hung on the horizon. Its light was starting to change the cold blue ice fields on Mount McKinley to a pale rosy-pink.

Toklat and her family grazed slowly away from the beaver pond and up the rough tundra, where the hundreds of caribou trails ran toward the sun. Toklat's nose still bothered her, and Chocolate's paw made traveling difficult. He trailed behind, whimpering, but his mother paid no attention.

In a field of dwarf birch, Toklat stood upright as the scent of other bears reached her. Pointing her nose into the wind, she saw the grizzly family.

Several hundred yards down the hill, the twin mustard-colored cubs and their mother were feeding in a patch of vetch. The herb's pealike blossoms were beginning to form, giving the slope a pale purple cast. The grizzlies were eating blossoms, leaves, and roots.

The soft sound of bushes being crushed reached the mustard-colored family. Rising in unison, the mother and her twins stood erect on their hind legs.

It was Kluane, limping slowly through the dwarf birch toward them. The cubs watched the great grizzly approach. Here was a time of decision — to stay at their mother's side where they had always been protected, or put the safety of distance between them and this strange bear.

When Kluane was fifteen feet away, he half rose, half leaped toward the cubs and swung at them with his good front leg. The cubs did not hesitate. They raced into the draw and did not stop or look back until they were several hundred feet away.

Kluane came closer. The rust-colored female did not turn away. They touched noses, then separated. With necks arched and heads low, they circled each other, talking in a huffing, puffing monotone. The female spun around and loped over the hill. Kluane followed.

The twin cubs raised their heads and watched their mother disappear. Her departure was not unexpected. For a month she had been weaning her cubs and encouraging them to forage for themselves. And, now, their family ties were finally severed.

Toklat and her family, watching them from the slope above, had seen a preview of their own destiny — the day when two-year-old cubs enter adulthood.

The sun had dipped below the horizon an hour ago, but its rays still illuminated the upper glaciers of Mount McKinley. In midsummer there is no interval of darkness to separate evening from morning.

For days, scattered herds of caribou had been crossing the Toklat Valley. The groups had numbered from a dozen to three hundred animals. Today the largest band of the season was wandering westward. It was really two herds that had united near the headwaters of the Sanctuary River. The larger herd had spent the winter near Lake Minchumina, two hundred miles to the north. The smaller herd had wintered in the Susitna River Valley near Broad Pass. Two months ago the warm spring sun had sent both herds into the high country, seeking the new food exposed by the melting snow.

The caribou kept no schedules. Their unpredictable movements were dictated by food, by weather, and by insects. During the heat of the day, they assembled and moved in tight herds to escape the warble flies. Pestered and preyed upon, they are forced to wander constantly. Orphans of the tundra, they have no restricted area to call home. Unchanged since the Stone Age in their appearance and habits, their species has survived because of this restless wandering habit.

The large herd surged over the trails directly below Toklat. Lying on her back, nursing her cubs, she watched a cow walk away from the others. Minutes later the caribou dropped her calf and cleaned the small pile of wet fur with her tongue. As the new calf dried, his coat became a deep red-ocher color, and his muzzle black.

The mother's fur was much lighter. Poised delicately between her ears, she carried a small pair of slender antlers with short, stubby brow tines.

The little calf tried to stand, but lost his balance and flopped to the ground. His second attempt was better and he succeeded in poking his black nose under his mother's front leg. Feeling his way down her side, he soon found the nipple and had his first meal.

A hundred yards away, two other cows stood with their new calves beside them. One walked to a patch of purple-blue lupine, her tottering calf following awkwardly. The new mother led her baby toward the two other cows. A mobile nursery was forming.

When most of the caribou had moved out of sight, the

mothers become restless, for this was a time of intense hazard for them. They needed the protection of the herd.

Another wave of caribou flowed over the ridge near Toklat. They were following the trails that had been etched into the hillside over the years.

Toklat could hear the low, grunting conversations of the calves and cows. She stood up, scattering the cubs, and watched the approaching herd. She was upwind from the caribou, and her scent drifted across the tundra. When it reached the lead cow, she stopped and looked up at the bears. Holding her nose high, she dropped her small antlers back close to her shoulders. This was her signal to the herd and it raced from animal to animal. All walking stopped.

Toklat sprang toward the herd.

The caribou reacted as a unit. They did not scatter, but altered their direction slightly, running down to the caribou nursery.

Toklat's long leaps carried her effortlessly over the grassy hummocks. Buttercup and Straw-Tan stood on their hind legs, but Chocolate, still bothered by the porcupine quills, sat and watched.

The high-stepping herd was now in full flight. In seconds they enveloped the nursery cows. Toklat was not far behind. When the herd passed beyond the nursery area, the newest mother was left behind with her calf.

Toklat's galloping pace did not change. As she drew close to the cow, the distraught animal snorted, shook her head, turned and ran a few steps, then stopped and looked back. Her calf struggled to his feet and stood unsteadily. Toklat, leaping, pinned the calf in the grass with her front paws. Her tongue hung out and she panted rapidly as she watched the calf's mother standing helplessly a short distance away.

Toklat rested a minute, then picked up the limp animal in her mouth and walked slowly back to her cubs.

Autumn

The first light of morning glowed through the ceiling of gray clouds that covered the sky. As the sun rose higher, the clouds brightened, and soon it forced its rays through a sparse opening. A streak of orange formed and slowly expanded, scattering a transparent fan of light onto the tundra. As the clouds moved, the rays followed like a giant searchlight. Where the beams struck, they illuminated masses of brilliant fall colors. The tundra's carpet of green had changed to golden yellows, reds, and deep russets.

The autumn night had been cold. The water along the quiet edges of the beaver pond carried sharp ice splinters. Thin and glasslike, they surrounded the slender shafts of grass that stuck up stiffly through the figured crystal. Along the edges of the streams, where the water slowed, thin shelves of ice pried cautiously into the current.

During the summer, Toklat and the cubs had wandered freely through her home area. They had grazed up onto the foothills north of the main range. They had made many crossings of the valley and had climbed high enough to find snowbanks in the shadow of the ridges where they were hidden from the warm sun of the long Alaskan days. At times, the cubs had curled up to nap on the cool snow, to escape from flying insects and to wait while Toklat was hunting among the nearby marmot colonies. They had no regular bedding areas.

Toklat's nose had been sore for a month after her

encounter with the porcupine. The quills, which had broken off, had left their barbed points deeply embedded. These had festered, but when the barbs finally dropped out, the sores healed. The quills in Chocolate's paw had gone through the same slow process. Now, three months later, he could walk without limping.

Toklat and the cubs had spent the night on a small rise on the south side of the valley, in a grove of black spruce trees.

The morning light, and a noise in the willows near them, aroused Straw-Tan and Buttercup. Chocolate slept quietly against his mother's side. Straw-Tan yawned, rose to her feet, and looked toward the sound.

The view of the valley before her was framed by two big trees. Beyond, in a clump of thick brush, a flock of willow ptarmigan chattered noisily. Straw-Tan followed the sound with her ears as the birds dashed through their tiny forest of willow brush. When the first bird walked into the open, neither bear showed any surprise. Soon several birds appeared and plucked at a cluster of drying blueberries.

The ptarmigan were acquiring their winter plumage of white, and carried only a few dark remnants of their summer coats. Their feet were covered with feathers that would act as snowshoes as they walked over the deep winter drifts. The black outer feathers on their tails would remain unchanged.

Straw-Tan watched the busy birds with increasing interest. When she could resist no longer, she proceeded slowly in their direction. Buttercup watched for a moment, then trailed close behind. The cubs made no attempt to stalk and were quickly seen.

Several of the ptarmigan crouched low as they scuttled quietly through the bright-colored branches. Others sank down into the brush and grass, hoping to be unseen against the mottled background.

Straw-Tan and Buttercup continued their curious ambling pace, sniffing and swinging their heads from side to side.

Suddenly one of the birds lost his courage and shot into the air with a low rasping whine — "whirrr." In seconds the entire flock catapulted into the sky. A high-pitched sound came from the birds as hundreds of feathers whistled with every stroke of their wings. The flock banked in a wide circle and disappeared over a knoll.

The morning sun soon lost its small peephole through the cloud bank as a heavier mass rolled up from the horizon. A brisk breeze stirred through the leaves and branches, carrying the first snowflakes. The tiny crystals dipped and swirled, then lodged daintily on the leaves' bright-colored surfaces. Others were captured in the slender fingerlike needles of the evergreens. Soon the air was full of the hurrying flakes, responding to every whim of the irregular, blowing currents. The snowstorm gradually deposited a thick frosting of white over everything. The flakes settled on the bears' long fur, giving them a soft white mantle over their backs.

As the storm increased, the visual world around the animals shrank. The grizzly family worked its way across the valley, fording several streams and leaving a well-marked trail in the new snow. As they fed closer to the lake, they found exposed patches of lowbush cranberries hugging the ground. The cubs playfully competed for the red berries by hurrying from patch to patch. They had nursed during the night, but had begun to mimic their mother's ways and to sample some of the food she was eating.

Straw-Tan and Chocolate found a dense cluster, but Chocolate resented sharing the berries and charged at Straw-Tan. The two bears rolled together into a ball of fur, snow and flying legs. Squealing and howling, they tussled for a minute, then separated with their customary huffing and puffing.

Toklat showed no concern over the squabble and continued to graze through the storm.

Chocolate, pawing a clump of berry roots, disturbed a mouse. It raced out of the fallen leaves and sought an escape tunnel. The cub pounced on the tiny rodent, pinning it to the ground. He picked it up with a lick of his tongue.

The cubs had grown rapidly during the summer. They were about eighteen inches tall and looked roly-poly beside their mother's four-foot-high shoulders. They were all fat and their fur had become a deeper color.

As the family grazed, they climbed a slope that led to the high cliffs where the Dall sheep had summered. Because of the storm, Toklat could not see the hills above her. The snow was a warning of the approaching winter. She knew instinctively that she must find a den for her family.

At the base of a ridge, she stopped in a spruce grove. Finding two large trees uprooted by the wind, she explored the rough, cluttered cavity beneath them. The cubs were still curious about their mother's every move and tried to follow her into the hole. Chocolate succeeded in squeezing into the space beside his mother, but Straw-Tan and Buttercup could only plug the entrance. Their round furry hindquarters were left in the snow. Toklat endured the pile of cubs for several minutes, then backed out with a roar, tumbling the cubs away from the sheltered hollow. Stepping under a heavy bough, Toklat slumped onto her side and allowed the cubs to nurse.

By midmorning, drifts of snow covered the irregular ground and tapered sharply behind every large rock. Toklat, still looking for a den site, returned to the bed of the Toklat River. The watercourse was almost dry and only a small stream cut a black, jagged pattern through the center. The bears waded through the water and climbed the bank. The slope ahead was especially familiar. A hundred feet above them was the den where the cubs had been born.

The wind swept the snow past them in a swirling gale, limiting their vision. Their heavy bodies sank through the fresh snow as they climbed toward the den's entrance. Ten feet from the old den, Toklat stopped, rose on her hind legs, and sucked in a faint odor. Moving to the entrance, she found that the strong scent was coming from the den. Toklat had no need to go farther; the smell told her enough!

The old bear Kluane had found the den two days before. Curled up in the snug chamber, he was asleep.

Toklat puffed a warning to the cubs and they galloped together back into the valley.

By noon the wind had weakened and only a few scattered snowflakes fluttered slowly to the ground. Searching along a high bluff near the river's edge, Toklat found an old wolf den. She stuck her head into the entrance and her sense of smell told her that this site was unoccupied.

Satisfied with the location, Toklat began enlarging the cavity. She had little trouble. The first freeze had barely penetrated the ground and her powerful front legs sent the dirt and rocks flying out behind her. She rolled the larger stones to the edge of the cliff where they cascaded wildly down the steep hill, scattering the snow from the bushes. Soon the hole was big enough to hide her body completely. The constant flow of rocks and dirt hurling from the entrance warned the cubs to stay away. They poked about through the snow, seeking the last few berries of the season.

The caribou herds were re-entering the valley and moving eastward over the tundra below Mount McKinley. Near the riverbed, an occasional animal stopped to browse on the willow brush.

As Toklat dug inside her den, a herd of several hundred caribou walked onto the river bar below her and splashed into the small, snow-fringed river.

This was the rutting season and the bulls traveled close to the herds. Their antlers looked like thin, outstretched arms with odd angular fingers on the ends. A single brow tine projected forward, almost touching the nostrils. A few of the animals' antlers still carried the last shaggy remnants of velvet, beneath which a deep reddish tinge was exposed. All the caribou had grown new coats of reddish-brown hair. The bulls, darker than the cows, had large collars of white hair around their necks, tapered down to thin white lines along their sides.

Near the rear of the herd were the old and crippled animals. A cow bobbed up and down, favoring an injured front leg. She was trying desperately to keep up with the herd while her leg healed. She knew instinctively that this was her only way to survive.

The caribou seldom walked. They were always in a hurry. The only peace they found was in moving. Trot — trot — trot — hurry — hurry — hurry!

On the cliff above the caribou, the pile of debris from Toklat's den cascaded down the hill in a slender plume — a long brown patch surrounded by new snow.

The cavity was now about six feet deep. With the strong nails on her front feet, Toklat continued clawing the earth and stones from the wall in front of her. Backing out slowly, she worked the loose rubble toward the exit. She paid no attention to the rocks and dirt that dropped onto her back with every passage back and forth.

At the inner end of the tunnel, Toklat uncovered a large boulder. Pulling it backward with her front feet, she worked it toward the exit.

Buttercup was climbing up the fresh dirt as her mother emerged with the rock. Giving it a tremendous swipe, Toklat pushed it over the brink. For a second it slid, then tipped and started an erratic plunge to the valley. Buttercup saw it coming and lunged out of its path. The rock's speed increased and it bounded like a live thing.

Chocolate and Straw-Tan were wrestling in a clump of dwarf birch. Neither animal was aware of the rock until it was nearly on them. Chocolate saw it first and scrambled aside. Straw-Tan saw only a fleeting shadow flying at her and she clawed the ground in an effort to escape. Too late! The rock struck a sharp blow on her hip and sent her rolling down through the brush. The cub bellowed in alarm and kept up the squealing until she came to rest against a small spruce tree.

Toklat heard the cry of distress and her reaction was immediate. She slid down the dirt to Straw-Tan's side and stood upright, looking for the enemy. Seeing the caribou in the valley, she watched them for a moment, then dropping back onto all four feet, she voiced a deep-throated command to the cubs to follow her.

With a swipe of her front paw, Toklat knocked the snow from a clump of blueberry bushes and fed on the fruit. For the present, the den-making was forgotten.

Straw-Tan whined softly, but Toklat paid no attention to her. She had answered the cub's cry of alarm, but since there was no enemy in sight, nor scent of danger, she resumed her normal habits. Protection for the cubs she would provide, playing she occasionally enjoyed, but humoring was no part of her natural behavior.

Chocolate and Buttercup followed immediately, but Straw-Tan, covered with dirt and snow, sat dejectedly behind the spruce tree. Not wanting to be left, she shook the dirt from her back and limped after her family.

Beyond Toklat and the cubs, a herd of caribou appeared over the ridge. At the sight of the bears they were frightened. They turned in unison and ran in a tightly packed group away from the grizzlies.

©LDassow85

As they trotted along the riverbank, two bulls suddenly stopped and lowered their heads into a fighting position facing each other. They came together with a hollow, cracking sound. For seconds they sparred and fenced with their antlers intertwined. Retreating and charging again, their antlers clattered and rattled as they struck against each other. Their footwork was light and agile as they circled and shoved and parried.

A red fox, startled by the sound, darted out of a blueberry patch ahead of them and loped across the snow.

The shoving, shifting contest of the two bulls continued, but with each circling thrust the smaller animal was pushed backward.

Minute after minute they battled, with their noses often dragging in the snow-covered tundra. The larger caribou soon had all the advantages. Pushing forward, he forced the young bull to retreat. Then, as the younger felt his way with his back feet, he suddenly lost his footing. With his hindquarters sprawled, he pawed out with his front feet. He was pinned to the ground! For a moment the old bull worked his hind legs in an arc around his fallen enemy, then tried to step back. His opponent's head followed each twist and turn. The heavy brown tine of the smaller bull was wedged securely at the base of the larger animal's antler. The ridged, fingerlike spikes of their antlers were firmly locked together.

As Toklat plodded up the slope, another herd of caribou moved into the valley. Abandoning their trails, they spread out over the tundra. Each caribou, widely separated from his neighbor, stopped momentarily to paw through the fresh snow and feed on the lichens beneath.

Above the caribou, at the top of the bluff, the large black male wolf and his yearling pups sat watching the valley. Behind them in the den, the mother snuggled her young pups to her side.

The father and older pups sprang to their feet and hurried down the bank. From twenty feet away, the two other adults joined them. When the pack emerged onto the open tundra, they were behind the caribou. With their leaping, bounding pursuit, they quickly closed half the distance between themselves and the herd.

Seeing the wolves, the caribou reacted instantaneously and swung into their high-stepping pace.

The bulls with their locked antlers were directly before the herd. The small bull regained his feet but both caribou were tired and made only a weak attempt to struggle apart. When the frightened herd enveloped them, they made a few staggering movements to follow. Their antlers would not separate! In seconds they were left standing alone in the path of the wolf pack, locked to each other.

Toklat, followed by the cubs, grazed on the brush tops that pierced through the snow.

At the top of the bank, Chocolate settled onto his hindquarters and slid down the hill. Buttercup was quick to follow. Straw-Tan limped up the hill but made no attempt to join in the fun.

In the late afternoon, Toklat and her family wandered back to the new den. Chocolate and Buttercup raced to the entrance, where they stood, heads extended, sniffing the earthy odors. Straw-Tan arrived and, for a moment, the three cubs plugged the opening. Chocolate, with a surge of courage, squeezed forward into the dark tunnel. Buttercup and Straw-Tan turned to watch Toklat climb up the last few feet.

Deep in the cavity where the boulder had been, a rock hung in the ceiling, held by a wedge of soft shale. Chocolate explored the end of the cave and with his front legs braced against the wall, poked his nose along the ceiling. The rock needed only this slight contact to loosen it and it dropped on the cub's head. With a bellow of surprise, he jumped back toward the exit. He made his huffing, puffing sound of anger. Hearing Chocolate's cry, the other cubs turned and bounded away from the imaginary enemy. Toklat was almost to the den when the cubs fled past her. She rose on her hind legs. Thrusting her head forward, she was ready to fight.

Frightened, Straw-Tan and Buttercup leaped several steps down the slope, then tried to stop their plunge by flattening their bodies in the snow. With the third leap, Straw-Tan's already injured muscles refused to obey. She lost her balance and rolled down the hill into a cluster of dwarf birch. She lay there a moment — a ball of furry dirt and snow.

Toklat, seeing or smelling no cause for alarm, entered the den. At its deepest point, she began enlarging the sleeping area.

The sound of the earthquake was only a whisper, but Toklat's sensitive ears heard it. She stopped digging. As she turned her head to the light in the opening behind her, the earth beneath her feet moved violently back and forth! A shower of rocks dropped onto her. Three feet in from the exit, a huge chunk of the tunnel's ceiling dropped, leaving only a peephole of light. Toklat shrank back into her nest cavity. Seconds went by. Another shock loosened more dirt and the peephole almost disappeared. Toklat waited, alert. She needed a familiar sound or odor to restore order to her suddenly shattered world.

The violent movements of the ground and its accompaniment of sound panicked the cubs. Shrill shrieks of terror came from the group. Buttercup was the first to gain back a measure of composure. With a few short leaps she was at the den's entrance and climbed to the top of the rubble. Another spasm of shakes loosened a shower of small rocks onto her. Buttercup recoiled and galloped past Chocolate and Straw-Tan, who stood on their hind legs looking for Toklat.

For the first time in their short lives, the cubs' mother was nowhere to be seen. Cries and squeals came from first one cub, then another, then they all joined together in sending a chorus of distress across the river bar and into the hills.

Kluane felt the quake, too. The walls of the older den, where he was sleeping, had dried and hardened, but the few pebbles that dropped were an annoyance. He sprang to his feet and jumped toward the exit. The walls of the tunnel met him at every step and tossed him back and forth. He emerged onto the small snow-covered ledge. Rocks cascaded down the slope on both sides of him. Bewildered, he turned his head from side to side as the earth under his feet continued to move. He staggered a step or two and sat down.

The falling snow limited Kluane's vision, but he heard the distant crying of the cubs and started out in the direction of the sound. He walked stiff-legged part way down the steep hill as if trying to hold himself back, but as the grade of the slope lessened, he broke into an awkward gallop.

Chocolate and Straw-Tan clambered onto the pile of dirt blocking the entrance. With every breath they sent out urgent calls for their mother.

For imprisoned Toklat, only a tiny glow told where the opening had been. Sitting in the darkness, she heard the cubs bawling. With a violent shrug, she crawled to the vent hole and half growled an answer. Then she started digging.

Outside, Buttercup sat dejectedly a few feet from the clogged den. Looking up, she saw Kluane rushing down toward her. She stood on her hind legs, trying to see more clearly through the falling snow.

The huge bear was almost to Buttercup when he saw her

rise up before him. He, too, stopped and rose onto his hind legs. No mother's challenging roar greeted him as he twisted his head in a half circle. Buttercup turned to escape down the bank. Her movement was all Kluane needed. He charged after her.

Passing a few feet from the den's entrance, he plunged down the bank. Before him, Buttercup rolled and tumbled through the snow. In seconds Kluane had almost closed the distance between them, but their momentum carried them onto the river bar.

Buttercup tried to roll onto her feet — but too late! Kluane's jaws closed tightly on the loose fur of her neck. He shook her violently from side to side. When he stopped, she kicked her legs out and Kluane repeated the sharp twisting motion. When he felt no movement from the cub, he dropped the small body into the snow and walked back up the hill.

Buttercup lay very still. A thin sprinkle of snowflakes quickly formed a cloak over the little figure.

Chocolate and Straw-Tan silently hugged into the vent opening as Kluane limped by. They could hear their mother's huffing as she cleared a path through the fallen earth inside the tunnel. Her six-inch-wide front paws sent rocks and dirt flying backward. In minutes she touched the noses of her two fearful cubs and seconds later she had enlarged the hole to allow her to exit. She crawled out on her belly and stood up. With a rolling shake she flung the dirt and pebbles out of her fur.

Chocolate and Straw-Tan, crying, moved up to her, but stopped when Toklat coughed a warning. Kluane's passing had left a scent trail along the ridge and Toklat recognized it as a menace to her cubs.

Seeing Kluane's large, indistinct outline through the snow, she charged angrily up the bank. Kluane turned to meet her.

They came together with their mouths locked and their heads twisting and turning. Then they stood upright, fighting with their front paws. Long strings of foamy saliva dangled from their jaws. Toklat was the smaller of the two, but she was younger and stronger. For several minutes they tussled with Kluane weakening under Toklat's youthful strength. Suddenly he backed away and stopped. The two bears stood with their heads at a sharp angle to their bodies and faced each other. A low menacing roar came from their throats, but neither made a move to resume the battle. Kluane was the first to turn. Slowly he walked away from Toklat, leaving a trail of blood in the snow.

Toklat dropped onto her belly with her front legs extended. Turning the sole of her right paw upward, she licked at the snow that had packed between her toes. She repeated the same cleaning on her left paw.

Returning to the entrance of her den, she found Chocolate and Straw-Tan quietly waiting. Toklat turned her head to follow the sound of a wolf call, then she pushed through the clogged entrance and crawled into the small opening. Behind her, Chocolate and Straw-Tan paused a moment in the darkness, then tagged after Toklat. They were spending their first night in their winter home.

The events of the hour were not embedded in Toklat's memory. The earthquake and fight were only problems of the moment and quickly forgotten. Satisfied with the presence of cubs by her side, she was not aware of the loss of little Buttercup.

The snowstorm gradually passed and the rugged foothills and contours of Mount McKinley appeared through the cold blue blanket of night. Soft air currents tried to pry the thin line of the snow from the tops of the branches, but only a few of the loose flakes fluttered silently to the ground.

Across the valley a wolf song reached into the night.

The next morning the sky over the Toklat Valley resembled a vast clear dome, resting on the surrounding peaks. In the west the full moon had a tiny bright star to help it greet the day. The sun's rays touched the rounded peaks of Mount McKinley with pink, crept across the snowfields and glaciers, and found the new snow on the ridge above the den where Toklat and her family slept. The rays had not yet reached the den's entrance when Toklat's head appeared. Her warm breath sent plumes of frozen vapor into the cold air, where it hung about her head for a second, then disappeared. Her tongue lolled out and her jaws worked up and down as if tasting some airborne morsel. She crawled forward, stood up, and shook the dirt from her fur. Turning, she attacked the pile of debris that the quake had dropped in the entrance. Stopping for a moment, she listened to the sound of her cubs back in the den, then resumed digging. Before she finished, the sunlight had passed the ridge and reached the floor of the valley. She called her cubs. Straw-Tan emerged, blinking her eyes from the glare of the sun. Chocolate was close behind her.

Toklat and the cubs ambled down the bank, crossed the riverbed, and searched for food along a sunlit slope.

On a high cliff, a golden eagle watched the movements of the animals in the valley below. Like his neighbors the Dall sheep, he depended upon his eyes for information about the community. He could see the arrowlike crinkle of waves where the beaver was swimming through the pond. The caribou herds appeared antlike as they trotted over the tundra. On the far hill, across the Toklat River bar, he saw Toklat and her cubs walk out of a long shadow and stop in the sunlight. From somewhere below, the shrill whistling call of a hoary marmot reached him.

The huge bird shook out his feathers, extended his wings, and soared slowly into the valley. His aerial maneuvers were executed with beauty and effortless grace. He used every ascending air current to carry him out over his hunting area. His only exertions were the adjustment of his tail feathers and the slight extending and retracting of his wings. His long, carefully maneuvered glide brought him closer and closer to Toklat and the cubs. He saw her stop at the entrance to a ground squirrel's tunnel and start digging. The eagle soared in circles and rough figure eights, and with each pass came nearer to the bears.

Chocolate dug deeper and deeper into the burrow.

Underground, the squirrel could hear the bear's heavy breathing mixed with the scratching, digging sounds. He raced away through his longest escape tunnel and stopped three feet from the exit.

Adjusting his wings, the eagle dropped lower.

Peeking out, the squirrel saw the grizzlies were a safe distance away. He leaped out of the hole and ran across the snow toward the entrance of another burrow.

The eagle saw the squirrel and dived. The soft "swooshing" sound of his wings reached the ground and the other cub looked up.

As he neared the fleeing squirrel, the eagle slowed his descent with several sharp downstrokes. The primary feathers on the tips of his wings looked like long fingers clawing through the air. He angled his legs forward and caught the squirrel with the talons on his right foot. Without a pause he climbed upward, carrying his victim, and disappeared behind a grouping of tall trees.

Only the cubs saw the eagle's successful hunt. Toklat, busy with her noisy digging, did not know that she had been outwitted by the ground squirrel and robbed by the eagle. She dug for several more minutes but, getting no encouraging scent, gave up the hunt.

Standing quietly outside the hole, she raised her head and

inhaled the crisp, cold air. Vapor hung about her nose with every breath. The freezing cold had sealed in the delectable odors of berries, grasses, and roots. Instinct told Toklat that soon her food sources would be gone.

With a soft rumble in her throat, she called the little bears and they walked along the top of the ridge which led toward Sable Mountain and the beaver pond to the east.

They grazed until the rosy glow on Mount McKinley had almost reached its crest. A low horizontal plane of clouds obscured the lower glaciers, which only moments before had also carried the pink cast of evening. The bear family lost all color, silhouetted against the light peaks.

In a grove of spruce, Toklat selected a tree and, backing up to it, rubbed up and down. When she finished she dropped to the ground and led the two hungry cubs to the rough den made by the upturned roots of a windfall. She stopped and checked the odors. All was acceptable and together they huddled into the shelter.

After Toklat's destructive visit in the summer, the beavers had found a temporary home under the roots of a tree at the pond's edge. They had worked on the wrecked lodge for a month, reusing many of the old sticks that Toklat had tossed aside. Wedging them firmly into the old walls, they had cemented them with mud. Trip after trip the beavers had waddled up the walls, carrying sticky bundles of mud with their front feet.

Day after day the lodge had grown and gradually a ceiling, with a rough vent, covered their quarters. By late summer, the beavers were again occupying their rebuilt home.

Today, the beavers woke in the early afternoon. The familiar sound of wavelets lapping gently against the lodge was not present. During the night, the surface of the pond had acquired a coating of ice, stilling the water. This was the silent signal of winter's approach.

Suddenly the cracking sound of breaking ice, and of water dashing and splashing, reached the beavers. They tried to fit the noise into a known experience but none could satisfy them. They would have to investigate.

The male slid quietly into the water pool in the center of the floor and swam downward. At the bottom he followed a channel in the direction of the dam. Surfacing carefully, he came up through a large break in the ice. A small chunk rode on his head and his nose pushed floating panes of ice before it. At the dam end of the pond, a cow moose and her twin calves were eating the willow brush that grew around the edge of the water. The moose

family had
moved from
the lake to
the beaver
pond the day
before, and they
were finding appe-
tizing food.

Browsing up
to the dam, the
cow had seen the
willow branches the beaver had used in construction. They
had sprouted and grown during the summer and looked very
tempting. Pulling a slender twig with her mouth, she had
stepped into the pond, shattering its surface and sending
jagged lines racing toward the beaver house. Some of the
glasslike ice fragments were tilted at sharp angles. Waves
of water from the moose's hooves rose and fell about the
beaver lodge.

The twin calves stood balancing on the rim of the dam.
They too were enjoying the small shoots, unmindful of the
slow destruction they were causing. With each mouthful torn
from the dam, a new trickle of water seeped into the break
and disappeared into the web of sticks. As they fed, the
trickles grew in size and soon several wide tongues of water
were dropping over the downstream side of the dam. The
sound of escaping water increased, and the beaver circled
closer and closer to the break and the monsters causing it.

The cow was uneasy, for this was the rutting season when

every moose sought a mate. A branch snapped in the brush behind her and she raised her head, cupping her ears toward the sound.

Suddenly the moose mother raised her muzzle and sent a low, hoarse call ringing through the air. Almost instantly a crashing in the willows told of the passage of a large animal. The cow's ears followed the sound until a bull moose appeared at the end of the pond. He had picked up her scent but needed her encouraging whine to lead him to her. Without hesitating she left the water and, with slow, powerful steps, walked out of the beaver pond. Water dripped from her long, angular legs and wet body, giving a shiny black appearance to her underparts.

As she approached the bull, she grunted. The bull answered with a hollow call, deep in his throat. Greetings over, the cow turned and walked away from the pond. With a shake of his heavy antlers, the bull followed.

The calves picked their way off the dam and, when they reached solid ground, trotted after their mother.

In the shadows along the pond's shore, wide, translucent panes of ice hung on slender shafts of grass as the water below them dropped.

When the moose had gone, the beaver, joined by his mate, worked for an hour stemming the breaks in the dam. Pushing through the thin, floating ice cakes, they made many trips to the brush-lined shore. Each time they returned they towed boughs of willow, or previously cut branches, the bark of which they had eaten.

When the escaping water was slowed to a trickle, the male returned to the problem of food. Near the pond's edge, he selected a cottonwood tree several inches in diameter, with an abundance of tender branches at its top. Rising on his hind feet, he placed one front foot above the other and started gnawing at the soft bark. He used his flat tail as a prop for balance. With each bite a large, curved wood chip dropped to the ground. Halfway through the trunk he stopped to listen. No strange sounds reached him. For a few seconds he ground his teeth together, sharpening their cutting edges, then he bent forward and peeled more chips. In a few minutes the work was finished and the tree swished into the broken ice. Walking into the water, he selected a place midway on the trunk and started another cut.

His mate joined him and, whittling one of the thinner branches from the top, she towed it to the food pile near the lodge.

The male quickly divided the trunk into two pieces. He grasped the top portion in his teeth and jerked it into the deeper area of the pond. With the surge of water into his mouth, soft folds of flesh came together behind his teeth, blocking his throat. This allowed him to carry the tree while submerged.

Towing the cluster of branches to the food pile, he passed his mate without a sign of recognition. There was no time for nose-touching now. His broad webbed feet shoved him through the water like a miniature tugboat. Stroke, stroke, stroke — left, right, left, right. Small pieces of ice swirled around him. A branch snagged on a sunken limb and the beaver gave two rough, impatient jerks with his head. It broke free and in minutes he was directly over his food cache. Arching his back, and with a new hold on the trunk, he dived to the bottom. He quickly wedged the trunk into the soft silt and rose to the surface. A partially sunken branch moving toward him was towed by his mate.

The gathering of their winter supply of food was almost finished. After a few more trips, they returned to their lodge to dry their wet and oily fur.

Under the unbroken ice at the far end of the beaver pond, a fish hung in the slow current. It was a five-pound Alaska trout with a brown-and-yellow body and an orange tinge on its sides. Above the fish the pane of ice held a few trapped air bubbles, which jiggled slowly toward the dam.

Suddenly a leaf fluttered across the surface in a gust of wind. The fish flashed upward, crashed through the ice and landed a foot from the hole. Angular chunks of ice scattered about the area. The fish's tail beat the ice with a violent tattoo. With each sporadic outburst of energy, the trout moved farther from the hole in the ice and closer to the shore. The rapid slapping of its tail slowed, then after a minute stopped. Arching its body against the ice, it lay still.

By midnight the water in the beaver pond had again reached the top of the dam. As the temperatures dropped, new long, sharp crystals formed. By morning a thick sheet of ice covered the pond, and a scattering of tiny snowflakes started to fall.

When the gray morning lightened, Toklat walked out of the protection of the log and stopped near the trunk of the rubbing tree. She stood quietly swinging her head, seeking a familiar odor in the flake-filled air currents. The snow landed on her eyelids and quickly speckled her fur with white. She sent an annoyed shrug through her body and turned toward the beaver pond.

Chocolate, as usual, was the first to follow. He dived after his mother with a series of quick leaps near her heels. Straw-Tan uttered a soft cry and hurried after them.

As the grizzlies approached the beaver pond, Toklat surveyed its changed appearance. The water had disappeared, and a coating of ice supported the snow which was forming into shallow drifts that tapered out from the shore. At the dam a small flow of water raced over the top through a tiny spillway. The speed of the water prevented the formation of ice crystals.

Suddenly a beaver's head rose out of the circular opening at the spillway. With his body in the water, he chipped away the icy edges of the hole with his chisel teeth. Pulling himself up onto the ice, he stood for a moment with his front legs against his chest in a prayerlike position. Dropping forward, he waddled across the ice to the shore, selected a small tree, and started gnawing. The thin trunk was cut almost through when a gust of wind sent it toppling to the ground. The uncut portion of the trunk broke with a loud snap.

Toklat heard the sound, saw the beaver, and charged. The beaver, alerted by the first crashing lunge of the bear, raced down the bank and onto the frozen pond. For the moment he could escape only by reaching the small black hole in the spillway. He ran rapidly toward it.

Toklat jumped on the ice ten feet from the beaver and crashed through. The surface cracked and splintered and the water swelled up through the openings. The beaver balanced a moment on a segment of ice, then slid backward into an unexpected avenue of escape that Toklat had unwittingly presented him.

The disappointed bear sloshed back among the ice floes, rejoined her cubs, and shook the water from her fur.

A red fox, hunting in the area, heard Toklat crash into the water, and ran to the pond. Two feet before him on the ice lay the frozen trout, now covered with a thin veil of snow. His nose picked up the fish's faint but appetizing odor and he stepped carefully to it. Pawing it loose from the ice, he carried the trout up the bank and settled down in the snow to enjoy his meal.

For Toklat, the storm was annoying but not confusing. She knew her territory well and headed back in the direction of her new den. Wading through the slowly deepening snow, she checked each tree. Finally she found one with

bits of bear fur clinging to it, and its upper trunk scarred with claw marks. She rose against it and, with her front legs stretched high, scratched deep gashes in the bark. This action completed, she resumed her journey, stopping frequently to check the wind scents.

The cubs, alternating between small leaps and a gallop, followed in single file through the trench that Toklat carved in the soft snow. They moved with their customary bear mannerism of glancing backward after every few steps.

Toklat knew she must retire with her family for their long winter sleep. She and the cubs were well prepared. Their rich diet had given them enough fat for their semihibernation. Their fur had grown long and heavy.

All day they trudged through the snow. By evening they were at the foot of the slope where Buttercup lay buried under a drift.

Toklat hesitated twenty feet below the den and tried to recognize a wisp of scent. Its source and identity eluded her. It was not man, not another bear, so she moved slowly toward the cave.

Toklat again picked up the scent, but the strong eddying winds still concealed its source. She rose with her hind legs far apart and tried to see through the snow.

A wolverine, inside the den, saw the bear's huge outline darken the exit and he reacted immediately. His heavy muscular body was close to the ground as he charged toward the grizzly. The wolverine burst through the narrow exit directly between Toklat's furry legs and plunged downhill.

Toklat had only a fleeting glimpse of the shape bounding away from her. She made a short leaping charge after it, but the wolverine quickly disappeared in the storm. Toklat shook the snow from her back and returned to the den. Chocolate and Straw-Tan waited near the entrance.

Toklat carefully sniffed the den's odors before walking into the darkness. At the end of the cavity she scraped several loose rocks from her bed area and settled back against the wall. There was no necessity to line the floor with sticks and grasses as she had the year before in preparation for the birth of the cubs.

With a soft sound, Toklat called her family. Chocolate, whimpering, was the first to respond. Straw-Tan pushed in behind him.

In the space of several steps, they walked from a chaotic world of howling wind and white, swirling snow into one of black silence. The reassuring sound of Toklat's huffing breath encouraged them to come to her.

The grizzly bears watched the faint circle of light at the entrance dim and then disappear as the day ended. Soon the heavy snow of winter would close the opening to the cave. Fat, safe and warm, Toklat and her cubs were content to forsake the cold outer world.

Winter

The midwinter night was ending. Over the Toklat Valley a full moon hung in the western sky as the first glow of morning tinted the eastern horizon. The valley and hills were still covered by a pale greenish light — the luminous moon color of night.

It was three months since Toklat and the cubs had entered their silent den. Buried under the snow, they were not conscious of the cycles of day and night, but in the valley other inhabitants were soon stirring.

The sun's first rays shot over the jagged peaks of the Alaska Range and gradually revealed the valley's smooth contours. A vast, undulating snow blanket covered the river's course and the grassy tussocks of the tundra, but the river and streams had left clues to their meanderings. Clumps of willow, aspen, and cottonwood outlined the banks, waiting for the spring floods to revitalize them. The trees' bare branches etched a delicate tracing against the sky. The tall evergreens kept their bold patterns — slender columns of deep green with irregular, dipping clusters of branches, outlined sharply against the white snow.

The morning sky was cloudless except for a mile-long streamer of snow particles which trailed from the tip of Mount McKinley forty miles away. The strong wind blowing across the peak carried the dustlike snow in a horizontal ribbon. When the sun's rays touched the soft banner, it acquired a warm pink hue. The mountain colored at the same time. The glow grew brighter as it flowed into the valley.

The sun's late arrival was a warning that this midwinter Alaskan day would last only a few hours. Rising obliquely above the ridges like a huge orange balloon, it sent an illusion of warmth over the landscape. The temperature was forty degrees below zero.

On the river bar below Toklat's den, a flock of ptarmigan had bedded down in a snowdrift the previous evening. When the first bird's head appeared, only his black eyes and a wisp of red comb were visible. The white feathers on his head were lost against the snow's brightness. A rough monotone clucking sound came from the bank and soon several more pairs of eyes appeared. The first bird emerged from the snow and only his shadow disclosed his size and position. The shadow rippled across the snow and left small, triangular footprints marking the bird's trail.

Soon a flock of thirty birds scampered away. Strings of footprints expanded in the powdery snow from the birds' wanderings. With their feather-covered feet, they raked away the snow from the bushes, seeking dried frozen berries. Others pulled the tips from the willow branches.

The ptarmigan were constantly alert for enemies that could be seen — the red fox, or the dark flash of a hawk.

Under a bush, near the birds, a pair of small black eyes watched intently. Twelve inches behind the eyes a black spear of fur twitched. The rest of the white body blended perfectly with the snow. This was an enemy that couldn't be seen — it was a weasel, wearing his winter coat of ermine.

Like the ptarmigan, only the weasel's shadow betrayed his position. His sinewy body twisted and turned as he stalked the nearest bird. Stopping in a slight depression, he stood high on his hind legs to observe his victim.

His fast charge was unseen. The six-ounce weasel caught

the twenty-four-ounce ptarmigan by the neck. For seconds the bird beat its wings in desperation.

As the weasel struck, the rest of the flock darted into the air. On the downward beat, their wings left a series of imprints in the snow. Flying near Toklat's den, they disappeared over the hill.

Their flight was not long. A half mile up the valley they circled over a new snowdrift. The first bird to leave the flock dived at top speed toward the snow. Inches above the surface he extended his heavily muscled chest and hit the snow with a soft "plunk." The force of the blow carried him a foot into the snow. He quickly worked the fresh snow from the walls and trampled it under his feet. His nest for the night was complete and there were no telltale tracks for a predator to find.

The rest of the flock followed him into the bank and only the soft "plunking" sounds accompanied their nest-building.

The birds had spent the short hours of daylight filling their crops with berries and tender buds. They were now ready to spend the long night in their snow dens, slowly consuming the undigested food.

On a low ridge below Polychrome Pass, the strong winds had kept some areas swept clean of snow. A flock of Dall sheep, feeding on one of these open slopes, had exhausted the supply of frozen grass and sedges.

Grazing to the edge of the cliff, the lead animal, a young ram, picked his way down the rocks to a snow-filled ravine. One by one the others followed. Soon the entire flock was working its way through the drift. The sheep made slow progress in their struggle across the deep, hazardous snow. Three hours after leaving the old ridge, the lead ram climbed onto the rocks at the edge of the new slope.

In the ravine which the flock had just crossed, an old,

sick ram floundered in the snow. Hours passed and his efforts became more feeble. By nightfall he lay exhausted, his body sunk deep in the drift.

The flock bedded down behind some large rock out-croppings and prepared to wait for the long night to pass. Each animal pawed the roughness from a small area and then, carefully bending first its front legs then its hind legs, settled slowly to the ground. There was little movement but that of alertness. A ram swung his head toward a suspicion of a sound. A ewe beside him cupped her ears in the same direction. There was nothing.

Above the tiny white sheep dots on the rugged landscape glowed the northern lights — a lazy curtain of gossamer streamers, fluttering as if propelled by a vast, gentle cosmic breeze.

After the male beaver's encounter with the bear, the pond's shattered surface had quickly refrozen, but the persistent beavers were not quite ready to surrender their pond to the long winter. At the crest of the dam, they were able to keep the small circular hole open by gnawing at its edges. They used this aperture for short trips to the snow-covered shore for food. They avoided the use of their submerged food pile whenever possible.

A week later the temperature was twenty degrees below zero. This was fifty-two degrees below the freezing point of water and a two-inch-thick plug of ice sealed the beavers' exit.

The beavers left their lodge and, following the bottom, swam to the hole. Gnawing and scraping accomplished nothing, and after several minutes they abandoned the effort to break through. Turning to the left, they swam slowly along the dam's rim. Minute after minute they probed along the undersurface where ice and sticks met, hopeful of finding another crack or vent that could be used, but the dam, spillway and pond's surface were frozen solid.

Suddenly their problem changed from one of food to a need for air. Trapped under the ice, they could drown. Ten minutes had passed since they had left their last air supply in the lodge.

The male, swimming with his nose pressed against the underside of the ice, found a large air pocket. When the ice had been cracked by the bear, ridges had formed, leaving air cavities. He took a quick breath and dived toward the submerged entrance of the lodge.

The water in the hole in the floor crinkled and rose slightly, then the beaver's head shattered the surface. His nostrils sucked in the much-needed air and, without pausing, he climbed up onto the rough platform and shook the moisture from his fur. In seconds his mate repeated the process beside him.

The marmot family had selected a thick jumble of rocks for a home. With the first freeze, they had crawled into the deep, grass-lined cavity. The beat of their hearts and their breathing slowed. In total darkness and silence, they had gone into hibernation. Nothing but the soft warmth of spring would waken them from their seven months of solitude.

The ground squirrel's sleep, like the marmot's, was true hibernation. He, too, had stored a bountiful supply of fat in his body and now rested unconscious and secure in his tunnel nest.

Down the valley, in Toklat's den of the previous winter, Kluane lay motionless. No vent hole showed in the surface snow to reveal the den's location. The old lean bear, with his wounds and worn teeth, had been unable to store up enough fat for his long sleep. He lay frozen in his tomb.

The wolf pack gathered on a low slope and exchanged the usual greetings. It was a tail-wagging, leaping assemblage, accompanied by an infinite variety of squeals, howls, and yipping. The greetings completed, the wolves trotted over the snow and onto the frozen Toklat River.

The pack now consisted of thirteen animals. The five yearling pups were as large as the older adults. Of the five pups born in the spring, four had survived.

The wolves, with their large, padded feet, traveled easily over the deep drifts, investigating every snowy depression and hummock. The wind had kept some of the areas free of snow. The pack paused a moment on a stretch of exposed tundra to sniff a pair of bare caribou skulls. The horns were locked firmly together. One of the pups tugged at a brow tine but quickly released it.

The pack loped in the direction of the high bank where Toklat and her cubs were sleeping. The snow had drifted high over the den's entrance and only the small vent hole gave a clue to its location. The warm air from the grizzlies kept the tiny hole open.

The big male wolf picked up a faint odor from the den and walked cautiously toward it. He knew the scent well and so made no attempt to dig. He bounded back to the pack and led them toward the crest of the ridge. The dry snow dented slightly with every footfall and a cloud of steamlike vapor hung about their noses. They all halted at the top of the hill and two of the wolves lifted their heads and sent a long, ascending howl into the bright moonlit night.

Overhead the greenish streamers of the Aurora Borealis shot upward in angular parallel shafts. The base of the ribbons appeared to emerge from a wide, flat, transparent plane. Each shaft moved by itself, shooting toward infinity, then suddenly dropping back into its source. The aurora was never still — writhing and twisting, its luminous base

crawled snakelike across the sky, suddenly breaking like an elastic band and snapping into a new curve.

In the den, the bears were not aware of the midwinter activity. The comforting nearness of the family group was all they needed. Chocolate and Straw-Tan had no reason for games or conflict — and so they slept on and on.

It was still three months to spring.

Appendix of Scientific Names

MAMMALS

Alces alces gigas	Moose
Canis latrans incolatus	Coyote
Canis lupus pambasileus	Wolf
Castor canadensis	Beaver
Citellus parryi ablusus	Ground squirrel
Erethizon dorsatum myops	Porcupine
Gulo hylaeus	Wolverine
Marmota caligata	Hoary marmot
Microtus oeconomus macfarlani	Mouse (tundra vole)
Mustela erminea arctica	Short-tailed weasel
Ondatra zibethicus spatulatus	Muskrat
Ovis dalli	Dall sheep
Rangifer arcticus stonei	Caribou
Ursus horribilis	Grizzly bear
Vulpes fulva alascensis	Red fox

INSECTS

Cephanomyia nasalis	Nostril fly
Oedemagena tarandi	Warble fly

BIRDS

Aquila chrysaetos canadensis	Golden eagle
Buteo jamaicensis calurus	Red-tailed hawk
Calcarius lapponicus alascensis	Lapland longspur
Lagopus lagopus alascensis	Willow ptarmigan
Larus canus brachyrhynchus	Short-billed gull (mew gull)
Nyctea scandiaca	Snowy owl
Oenanthe oenanthe	Wheatear
Pica pica hudsonia	Black-billed magpie
Stercorarius longicaudus	Long-tailed jaeger
Sterna paradisaea	Arctic tern

FLORA

Arctagrostis latifolia	Grass
Artemisia tilesii	Sedge
Astragalus	Vetch
Betula nana	Dwarf Arctic birch
Cladonia	Lichen
Cladonia rangiferina	Reindeer moss
Cornus canadensis	Ground dogwood (bunchberry dogwood)
Echinopanax horridum	Devil's club
Equisetum arvense	Horsetail
Eriophorum angustifolium	Tall cottongrass
Hedysarum alpinum americanum	Wild pea vine
Lupinus	Lupine
Oxytropis	Locoweed (oxytrope)
Papaver	Arctic poppy
Anemone parviflora	Anemone
Picea glauca	White spruce
Picea mariana	Black spruce
Populus tremuloides	Quaking aspen
Potentilla fruticosa	Cinquefoil
Dryas	Dryas (mountain avens)
Populus balsamifera	Cottonwood tree
Salix	Willow
Saxifraga tricuspidata	Saxifrage
Shepherdia canadensis	Buffaloberry (soapberry)
Vaccinium uliginosum	Blueberry
Vaccinium vitis idaea	Lowbush cranberry

About the Authors

Alfred and Elma Milotte spent more than three decades living among, photographing and writing about wild animals in Alaska, western Canada, the northern Rockies, the Florida Everglades, Australia, Tasmania and Africa. He was a commercial artist, she a teacher, when they were married. For five years before World War II they operated a photographic studio in Ketchikan, Alaska, then spent two years traveling and filming along what was to become the Alaska Highway. Walt Disney saw some of their footage and was inspired to begin his True Life Adventures series.

The Milottes' first Disney film, *Seal Islands*, was shot in 1946 on St. Paul Island of the Pribilofs. It was the first of their six Academy Award winners. That year, too, they filmed *The Alaska Eskimo* in Hooper Bay. They shot *Beaver Valley* in the northern Rockies, *Bear Country* in Alaska and Yellowstone National Park, *Prowlers of the Everglades* in Florida, and most of the footage for the composite pictures, *Water Birds* and *Nature's Half Acre*.

They spent two years in Australia and Tasmania, studying and filming the duck-billed platypus and its marsupial neighbors, which yielded footage for *Nature's Strangest Creatures* and copy for their first book, *The Story of the Platypus*, published by Alfred A. Knopf, New York.

Next came almost three years in Kenya, Tanzania, Zululand and South Africa, roaming in "Annie Lorry," the world's first mobile home — a four-wheel-drive vehicle built to their specifications to serve as living quarters and photography blind as well as transportation. Disney Studio's *African Lion* came from more than 50,000 feet of film exposed on that safari.

At Mzima Springs in Tsavo West, Kenya, the Milottes built an underwater viewing tank and worked in it for five weeks, watching and filming hippos as they never had been seen before. Countless later visitors were to spy on hippo life from a similar tank in that same spot, and the Milottes got material for their book, *The Story of the Hippopotamus,* also published by Knopf. Al did the sea gull photography for Alfred Hitchcock's thriller, *The Birds,* but "hated it because it made the birds hostile," he said. "Birds are not aggressive."

After doing a series of film lectures the Milottes built the dream house in which they lived, on a 128-acre hilltop in western Washington, with a full view of Mount Rainier. Al began painting (he had studied art at Cornish School in Seattle and the Chicago Art Institute), and in 1975 he had a successful one-man show at Seattle's Frye Museum.

Al and Elma Milotte had thirty years of more or less settled life in their dream home on Ehli Hill, sorting and cataloging literally miles of film and their vast collection of memorabilia from around the world. They donated their collection of Alaskan Eskimo and Indian masks to the Alaska State Museum in Juneau. Al painted in oils; Elma did some writing. She had bought a word processor and was working on the story of their joint life, when she died suddenly on April 19, 1989. Al, who had been in poor health in his later years, died five days later.

Many other fascinating books are available from
ALASKA NORTHWEST.
Ask for them at your favorite bookstore,
or write us for a free catalog!

ALASKA NORTHWEST BOOKS™
A division of GTE Discovery Publications, Inc.
22026 20th Avenue S.E.
Bothell, Washington 98021
CALL TOLL FREE 1-800-331-3510